MORE LIGHT

"I met Austin Shifrin through the Lodge in 2007 and immediately recognized a light within him that is not found in every Mason. Over the years, we have shared many conversations about the esoteric, the spiritual, and the mystical. . . I was pleased when he accepted my offer to become a regular contributor to *RiteNow*. . .

The articles compiled in More Light are at once heady and intellectual but at the same time conversational and familiar. He is equal parts storyteller and teacher. The paths he takes the reader on as well as the conclusions he draws will be both entertaining and thought-provoking to any student of the Craft."

Paul J. Roup
Right Worshipful Junior Grand Warden
Grand Lodge of Pennsylvania

". . . The title you are holding in your hands is the culmination of not only hours upon hours of writing, formatting and editing, but also of years spent honing his craft and expressing genuine appreciation of masonic brotherhood.

While reading his essays in succession, I was reminded of Carl Claudy's 'Old Tiler Talks' . . . the topics of each essay convey a wisdom greater than that of his years and experience. . .

I am proud of Austin for making these essays available to everyone, and I am proud for the fraternity having the privilege of counting him as one of its members. This book will be a valuable addition to any masonic library. I know it will be in mine."

Jason F. Craig
Grand Superintendent, Pennsylvania West
Grand Council, Allied Masonic Degrees

MORE LIGHT

COLLECTED MASONIC WRITINGS 2017-2021

AUSTIN R. SHIFRIN

Columbus, Ohio

More Light
Collected Masonic Writings 2017-2021

Published by Gatekeeper Press
2167 Stringtown Rd, Suite 109
Columbus, OH 43123-2989
www.GatekeeperPress.com

The cover design, interior formatting, typesetting, and editorial work for this book are entirely the product of the author. Gatekeeper Press did not participate in and is not responsible for any aspect of these elements.

Library of Congress Control Number: 2021952346
ISBN (hardcover): 9781662923791
ISBN (paperback): 9781662923807
eISBN: 9781662923814

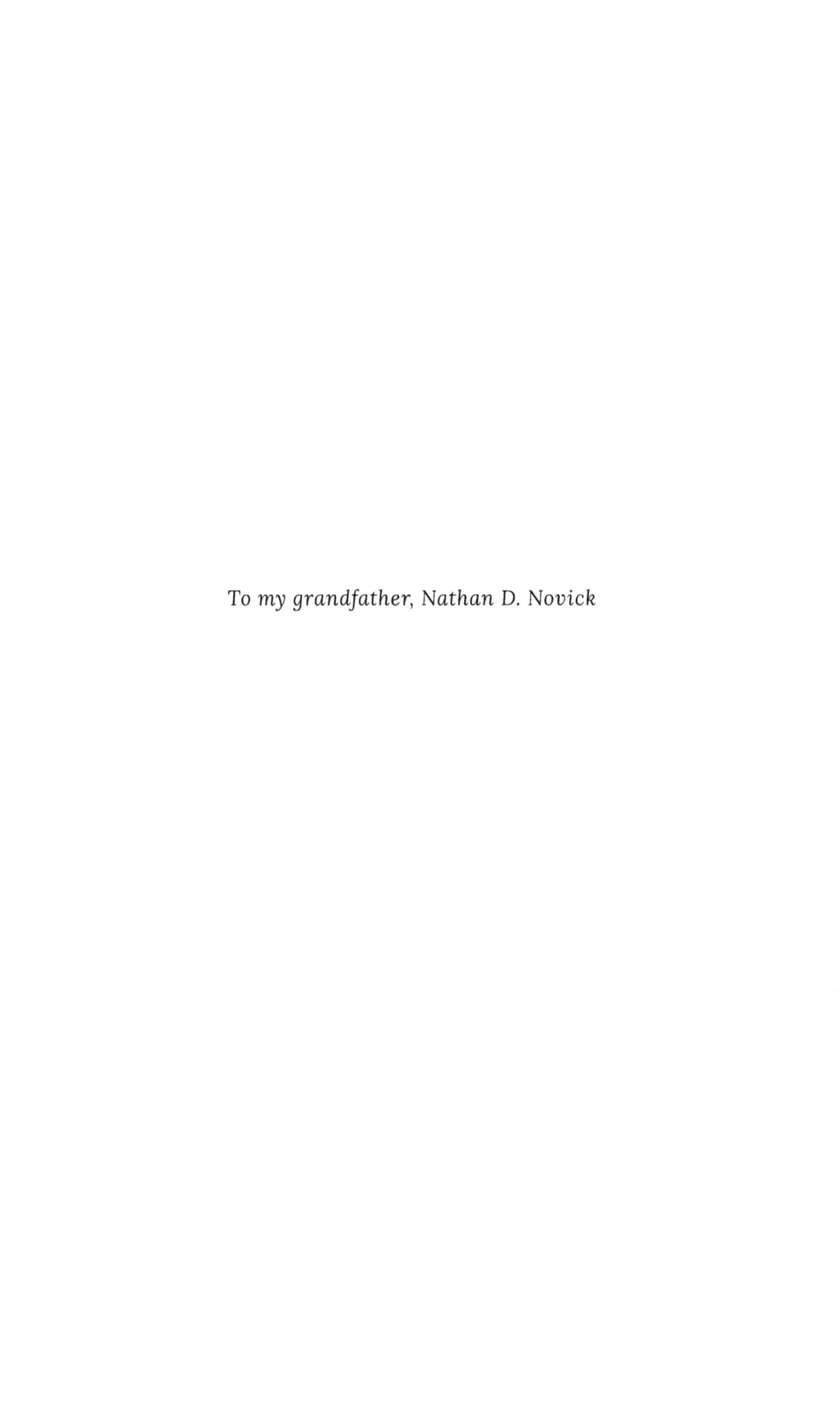

To my grandfather, Nathan D. Novick

Contents

The Banquet

Originally published in *RiteNow*, Vol. XXVII, No. 2, December 2017

When I saw the theme of this issue was to be "caring for each other," it brought to mind a tale that some brothers in the Valley of Pittsburgh have heard me tell before:

A certain Rabbi Haim of Romshishok had the opportunity to visit both heaven and hell, guided by an angel. On his journey to hell, he is surprised to encounter what appears to be a beautiful and sumptuous banquet. As he draws closer, he discovers that all the souls seated at the long banquet table have splints tied to their arms, so that none of them can bend at the elbow. As a result, none of them can eat, and he can hear their groans of frustration and suffering.

Upon his arrival in heaven, he is even more surprised to discover the scene before him seems strikingly similar: a long banquet table, set with many delicacies, and a great many people seated at the feast, all with their arms bound with splints, unable to bring a utensil to their own mouths. But among the residents of heaven he hears only happy and contented discourse, and as he draws nearer he discovers the difference: the souls seated at this banquet, are feeding each other.

Participating in blue lodge Masonry in Pennsylvania, or any of the appendant bodies, offers a great many opportunities for philanthropy. Calling cards and baby showers provided to military families, supported by our blue lodges; tutoring for dyslexic children sponsored by the Scottish Rite; the children's hospitals supported by the Shriners; and the summer camps for children with muscular dystrophy supported by the Tall Cedars of Lebanon all fill me with pride for the good deeds and impact we can accomplish in the world around us.

I am always impressed and humbled by the accomplishments of our Valley Hospitaler as well when I think of the countless hours and countless miles put in by Vito Urso (and brother Sammy Knappenberger before him). They have traveled far and wide, installing stairlifts and providing beds and other hospital equipment to our brothers in need, and have set an amazing example for any brother to look up to and emulate, truly embodying the vision that we should "strive to be a fraternity that fulfills our Masonic obligation to care for our members."

Amid all this naches, I admit there is a fact that still troubles me—how often we do not know that there are worthy brothers in need, out there suffering in silence. Maybe you, too, have experienced one of those embarrassing moments in your own lodge, a sudden revelation that someone who had not been seen or heard from in some time has been hit with some hardship—or worse yet, has passed on—without their brethren being aware of the circumstances.

I think the way to address this is twofold. One aspect is doing what we can to maintain or improve the communication between our Masonic bodies and our membership. You may be approached by an officer from one of the bodies asking you to help by calling on a few brothers now and then just to stay in touch; or the call may come in a more general form from an officer standing up in the body of a meeting looking for volunteers. Don't take one step backwards like one of the weaselly characters from *F Troop*. Step up proudly like one of the heroes of the Bible and say, "Here I am!"

The other aspect is that we need to get beyond the stigma that surrounds asking for help when we need it. We know that men are stereotypically bad at this, whether it is because we are fixated on our role as "providers," we feel obliged to be (or appear) tough, or we don't want to be objects of pity. I must argue that *we should have more faith in our brothers than to assume they will think any less of us for circumstances beyond our control.* In fact, even if we arrived at these circumstances due to our own flaws, a good brother is not going to scorn us; a good brother is going to remember that he is just as flawed as you are. Give him a chance to prove himself as a good and faithful servant.

As we move throughout our lives, then, let us always be ready to give care. And, maybe more so than we have been, let us be open and ready to receive care. And by this accumulation of our good deeds, big and small, let us make this world a fit dwelling place for the Grand Architect of the Universe by making it a brighter, happier, and more caring place for everyone else.

The Lewis Jewel

Originally published in *RiteNow*, Vol. XXVII, No. 3, March 2018

In an issue dedicated to family and Freemasonry, I thought it would be most appropriate to touch on the topic of the Lewis jewel. The Lewis is a jewel that may be worn by a man who is a Mason, whose father is a Mason. In the event that the father has passed on, the son still qualifies for this emblem if his father was in good standing at the time of his death.

As in most aspects of blue lodge Masonry, the jewel takes its shape and appearance from a tool used by operative Masons—tradesmen who work in actual stone—to convey a message through analogy and symbolism. The tool itself is easier to understand from an illustration than a verbal description. It essentially consists of three steel shapes, which can be suspended from a bolt through holes at the top of all three shapes that align together. The two outside pieces are wider at their bases than at the top, where the bolt passes through, and one piece placed in between acts as a spacer. The stone to be lifted is prepared by carving a hole into the top that widens as it deepens. The hole need only be as wide at the opening as the base of the two outer pieces of the Lewis side-by-side. Those pieces are lowered into the opening, then spread apart from each other until they abut the inner surface of the carved hole. The spacer is placed between them, and the bolt is run through the aligning holes at the top of all three pieces where they protrude from the stone. A crane, lever, or winch attached to that bolt can lift the stone. For a smaller stone, two men can carry a pole between them with the stone suspended from that. The approach is especially useful if the stone is too heavy to get a sling underneath it or if it has decorative protrusions that would prevent using some other device.

The device was invented by Greek engineers sometime between 200 and 300 BC, and they called it a holivela.[1] I was rather taken aback by this discovery since I have only ever seen or heard it referred to as a Lewis. However, I further learned that this distinction is helpful because there is a similar device called a split-pin lewis, a very clever variation. You must imagine a scenario with a similar hole carved into a stone that widens as it deepens. The split-pin lewis, being lowered into the hole, somewhat resembles a scissors, but with the handles intentionally bent farther apart. Those "handles" are connected to a single lifting implement so that when the lifting force is applied, they become closer together and the "blades" inside the stone separate farther apart, exerting force outward inside the tapered opening and making the device an effective anchor. There's a nice demonstration of this on YouTube posted by the Stonemasonry Department of the City of Glasgow College—I recommend you check it out.[2]

So, if the Greeks called it a holivela, where does the word "lewis" come from? As with several of our Masonic terms, the theories are varied and sundry. One inference is that it might come from the Latin word "levis," meaning light, which is the same root as our English word "levitate."[3] I think another strong candidate, just given its antiquity, is that the device appeared in architectural work in France in 1676 when Masons in the Compagnonnage called it a "louve," which translates to she-wolf, possibly referring to the grip of its jaws. Over time, this morphed into calling each of the wedges in the device "louveteaux," or male wolf cubs. And, just as contemporary Masons do, the Compagnonnage took care of the orphaned sons of its members, who were also referred to as "louveteaux." Did this term somehow further mutate into "lewis"? Sadly, we are left to speculate.[4] Still, another theory holds that it comes from a lineage dating back even further, in the ninth century Anglo-Saxon "leof-sunu," or "dear son."[5]

However the tool got its name, the intended metaphor of the lewis is, that as the tool may be used to lift the stone, so the efforts of the son ought to be to "support" their father. To be nitpicky for a moment, I feel like this is not the clearest metaphor for two reasons: one, when I think of the act of "supporting" I usually think of lifting from underneath rather than pulling from above; and two, the lewis does not itself do the lifting—that's done by the crane, lever, or winch—and the lewis is really more of an anchor or a grapple. But, my nitpicking aside, the sentiment is a heartwarming one and the symbol commemorates a beautiful elaboration on the relationship between father and son.

Use of the symbol in Freemasonry dates back quite far. In 1737, when it became known that a son would be born to the

Prince of Wales, a verse raising a toast to the new lewis was added by one brother, Gofton, to an existing composition called "The Deputy Grand Master's Song," and captured in a revised form in Anderson's *Constitutions* in 1738.[6] By 1801 the term appeared in the Junior Warden's lecture used in the Grand Lodge of England.[7]

Its use as a jewel began there and first arrived in the US in Pennsylvania Masonry.[8] Today, it is also utilized in Connecticut, Massachusetts, Montana, Texas, Vermont, Virginia, and in the jurisdiction of the Grand Lodge A.F. & A.M. of Canada in the province of Ontario.[9] What a fine thing that we have this distinct emblem to honor both the bonds of family and Freemasonry!

1   https://100falcons.wordpress.com/2010/08/27/how-did-they-lift-those-stones/

2   https://www.youtube.com/watch?v=_9T1rDF_oDo

3   R.W. Bro. Don Falconer, VII°, Second Grand Master Mason, Operatives Lodge #429, "The Lewis."

4   Bernard E. Jones, *Freemasons' Guide and Compendium* (Cumberland House, 2006), 417.

5   Leland L. Duncan, William H. Griffin, and Arthur William Hiscox, *History of the Borough* (The Blackheath Press, 1908), 18.

6   Jones, *Freemasons' Guide and Compendium*, 418.

7   http://thefleece.org/lewis.html

8   Jones, *Freemasons' Guide and Compendium*, 416.

9   http://thefleece.org/lewis.html

The Camp

Originally published in *RiteNow*, Vol. XXVII, No. 4, June 2018

If one is interested in symbolism in the Scottish Rite, there are many prospective sources from which to draw the light of inspiration; one might even argue there are too many. No matter how long one has to see all the degree work performed or learn the various words, signs, regalia, and batteries, we might reasonably observe that the Rite is truly abundant in its signs and symbols. It is perhaps because of this that one of its richest symbols, the camp, is sometimes overlooked.

I don't mean to imply that it is entirely overlooked. There was a lovely article on aprons in the May 2015 issue of *The Northern Light*[1] with an interesting sidebar regarding an unusual typo (if the term may be extended to embroidery) in which there is some discussion of the camp as it appears embroidered on a Scottish Rite apron. Similarly, a discussion of the same symbol embroidered on a Scottish Rite collar in MacNulty's *Freemasonry: Symbols, Secrets, Significance*.[2] Given that the author lived for some time in London, it is unsurprising to discover that the collar resides in the Library and Museum of Freemasonry in London. We likewise find discussion of the embroidered apron in *A Sublime*

Brotherhood, published by our own Supreme Council for the NMJ.[3] Given the common source between this and *The Northern Light*, then, it is also unsurprising to discover that these are both discussing the same apron in the collection of the Scottish Rite Masonic Museum and Library in Lexington, MA. What may interest some is that on closer inspection (of shadows and the arrangement of apron strings), it appears the two publications may have used the identical photograph—albeit the accompanying text in A *Sublime Brotherhood* makes no mention of the curious typo. Only *The Northern Light* article references "the tents and flags representing the divisions of the [symbolic] Masonic army."

Mackey's encyclopedia elaborates only slightly on the subject: "A portion of the paraphernalia decorated with tents, flags, and pennons of a Consistory of Sublime Princes of the Royal Secret, or thirty-second degree of the Ancient Accepted Scottish Rite. It constitutes the tracing board, and is worn on the apron of the degree. It is highly symbolic, and represents an imaginary Masonic camp. Its symbolism is altogether esoteric."[4]

At first I found this terse and unsatisfactory, but upon further review I appreciated the economy of language and what was implied between the lines: it *is* highly symbolic because it is a composite symbol intended to synthesize the lessons of all the degrees of the Rite and its symbolism *is* quite esoteric because one could not expect to cultivate an appreciation for this symbol without study and reflection on the preceding degrees.

I found a nice explication of the components of the camp in *The Book of the Ancient & Accepted Scottish Rite of Freemasonry*, where it is more explicitly expressed that the tents at the various sides and angles of the geometric figures that compose the camp represent the commanders—the spirits, if you will—of the various degrees, assembled in an orderly military fashion to advance the principles of Freemasonry.[5] The image resonates nicely for me when I consider it in the context of the motto, not of our 32nd, but the 33rd and last degree of the Ancient Accepted Scottish Rite: *Ordo Ab Chao*, or "order from chaos."

The tents make me think of the twelve tribes which originated with the twelve sons of Jacob (also known as Israel). I think tents and tribes are not a farfetched association. I often contemplate both how similar and how different lifestyles and interpersonal dynamics may be between that bygone era and now. I know that in ancient, nomadic, herding societies, trust and honor were easiest to extend to immediate family. Even aside from the most famous story of discord among those brothers, I begin to wonder whether, as they grew their own families and were responsible for more parties in their own formidable households, how that could have weakened their feeling of allegiance to the other tribes, at least in terms of wanting to prioritize their own. It would have taken a strong father, a strong nation, to make the center hold—to maintain order.

My mind next makes the associative leap between Ordo Ab Chao, a Masonic motto, to our American motto, *E Pluribus Unum*, or "out of many, one." We know this is in reference to the uniting of disparate colonies, or states, under a new federal body. Much as in the case of Jacob's sons, we know the states had sometimes divergent interests. It is only through the willingness to subordinate those interests to some greater good, some higher cause, that we have been able to, in the course of history, maintain our republic. We have succeeded in doing so through some very divisive times in our history. I hope and pray that we can continue to do so today.

Finally, and most relevant to this issue of "Light in the Rite," this sequence of thoughts brought me to one of my favorite pieces of language in blue lodge—when we make reference to persons being "refractory." Of course, we are using it in the sense of its dictionary definition as "stubborn and unmanageable." However, I think a valuable metaphor to deploy here is to think of the prism and what it does to light when it *refracts*: it takes white light and breaks it down into its component parts. When we act disparately, separately, we are representative of discord, we are behaving in a *refractory* manner. When we act together, as one united Masonic army, "out of many, one," we are representative of order and harmony.

So, if you enjoy looking at our Masonic camp as I do, at something like a mandala, inspiring this kind of chain of associations, I hope it will also lead you to thoughts of harmony and unity, as we labor together for a higher cause.

1   Aimee Newell, PhD, "The Badge of a Freemason: Scottish Rite Aprons at the Museum." *The Northern Light* (May 2015): 4-8.

2   W. Kirk MacNulty, *Freemasonry: Symbols, Secrets, Significance* (Thames and Hudson, 2006).

3   Richard B. Burgess, Jeffrey Croteau, Alan E. Foulds, Aimee E. Newell, Jerry A. Roach, Jr., and Catherine C. Swanson, *A Sublime Brotherhood: Two Hundred Years of Scottish Rite Freemasonry in the Northern Masonic Jurisdiction* (Supreme Council 33°, Ancient Accepted Scottish Rite, Northern Masonic Jurisdiction, 2013).

4   Albert G. Mackey and Robert Ingham Clegg, *Encyclopedia of Freemasonry* (Masonic History Company, 1946).

5   Charles T. McClenachan, *The Book of the Ancient and Accepted Scottish Rite of Freemasonry* (1868).

A Matter of Refinement

Originally published in *RiteNow*, Vol. XXVIII, No. 2, December 2018

There is clearly a long standing association we've made in our minds between Freemasonry and the term "gentlemen." In our modern comprehension we find it makes some sense because of the stated mission of Freemasonry to take "good" men and make them "better." So, it might seem intuitive that an organization that teaches dignity and refinement would be composed of gentlemen.

Even this simple perspective bears digging deeper into a bit. Just how important is refinement in the Masonic arena of self-improvement? After all, our discourse often refers to more profound notions of ethical and civic improvement; I think there is interesting gray area in the realm between ethics and etiquette. Consider whether it is a matter of ethics, or a matter of etiquette, to:

- Say "please" and "thank you"
- Bless someone when they sneeze (and do you feel differently about strangers than acquaintances)
- Hold doors for others
- Give up one's seat to someone disabled or inconvenienced on public transit

And then, to wade into minutiae, there is the aspect where etiquette blurs into protocol. How important is it, for example, that a man knows which utensils in a place setting go with which course in the meal? Or that he pairs the proper wine with the proper meat? But in the absence of more context, one might very well feel inclined to include even these latter things on a list of qualities indicative of "a gentleman."

There are linguistic aspects of this that are worth exploring further: we should remember that the term originates with Middle English in the early to mid-thirteenth century. The term "gentleman" once meant "a man of gentle (i.e., noble) birth, who was entitled to bear arms, ranking above a yeoman in social position." It also meant that because this man was a noble, he did not have to work a trade for a living. This has very specific implications, for instance, when the *Masonic Magazine* (vol. IX, 1881–1882) refers to Elias Ashmole as "the first known instance of an English 'gentleman' having been admitted into a lodge of what are generally believed to have been 'operative' Masons . . ."

I have often thought of this era and what an interesting but difficult transition it must have been.

The operative Mason included ethical and moral instruction in his teachings because the reputation of the guild as an entity depended on the conduct of its members. No one who had labored to advance the trade wished to see it besmirched by wayward behavior. Am I romanticizing it? I wasn't there in person so I cannot say. But how appealing it is to me to imagine these men striking that agreement: do not allow me to suffer by association with you, when all I want is for my skilled labor to have its own dignity.

Along come men like Ashmole, an academic, a botanist, a philosopher. A speculative Mason. Whatever his interest in the lodge is, he is not concerned with the literal experience of a craftsman in stone. And so, while conduct and public image may have mattered to him, that notion of being an ambassador of this guild, and being responsible for its reputation, may not have been foremost on his mind. And as the first nobleman, whatever he does hope to learn from this lodge, in the parlance of their time, there was nothing the existing members could teach him about being a "gentleman."

But the class distinctions of the thirteenth century in the UK are not our present reality, and the Freemasons of today are not those of yore. What we mean when we say gentleman, is "a civilized, educated, sensitive, or well-mannered man." And your blue lodge is a fine place to acquire these qualifications.

What makes a man civilized? Freud suggested that the foundation of civilization was impulse control. Part of lodge dialogue admonishes us about how we should govern ourselves and set boundaries. Other elements even specify how we should address a brother regarding his shortcomings, even at their most egregious, in a gentle manner. Surely, if we could adhere to this rhetoric, the world would observe how Freemasons would be uncommonly civilized.

What makes a man educated? I feel that Freemasonry's great challenge on this front is that you can lead a horse to water, but you can't make him drink. As you might infer from the preceding paragraph, I believe there's a great deal of wisdom captured in the dialogue of our ritual. I am not the first, nor the wisest, writer to remark that it's possible we become so anxious about memorizing the ritual correctly that we give insufficient time and attention to simply understanding it. But it's in there. I advocate that we set aside time to dissect and discuss ritual amongst ourselves for the advancement of this purpose.

What makes a man sensitive? Well, that's a loaded term. Today, as men, we may fear being labeled "sensitive" if we assume it a feminine or effeminate quality; and in the US, we may even attribute political overtones to it. But if sensitivity can be construed as empathy for your fellow then undoubtedly, we must learn sensitivity. We are called upon to imagine ourselves in another's position and treat him the way we would want to be treated; surely this is fundamental to the brotherhood of man, under the fatherhood of God.

What makes a man well-mannered? This is exactly where I feel we enter the gray area of etiquette, depending on how far into the minutiae I described earlier you wish to delve. On the one hand, we may believe that an extra level of polish is what distinguishes between someone who is merely nice and someone who is perceptibly a gentleman. On the other hand, is insisting upon the finer points of etiquette an elitist stance that undermines the egalitarian spirit of Freemasonry? If we're willing to agree that a well-mannered man could at least engage in simple acts of kindness—holding a door, giving up a seat, saying "bless you" when someone

sneezes—then perhaps the world will be pleasantly surprised
to see that gentlemen still walk among us.

What Makes a Traveling Man?

Originally published in *RiteNow*, Vol. XXVIII, No. 3, March 2019

I feel the need to begin by saying that I am highly conscious that my audience includes both people who are more experienced in Masonry than I am, and people who are less so. I am truly grateful for the gift you grant me in giving me this platform, and I hope that what I share can be enlightening to some, even if there may be others for whom what I reveal is not "news." After all, some of you have traveled this road much farther than I, while others have only just embarked upon your journey. So today, I would like us to truly confront the question of what makes a traveling man?

The metaphor of travel enters into a man's Masonic career at the very beginning of initiation. The presence of this symbolic journey in blue lodge results in the quaint, semi-secret exchange you will sometimes see between brothers who encounter each other in public, who are not yet certain of each other's membership; where one will inquire of the other, "Are you a traveling man?" The metaphor has then naturally been extended to appendant bodies, where we refer to "your Scottish Rite journey of a lifetime," or when we say one should continue one's journey from blue lodge to York Rite because of the links in the content.

I suppose I could be more discriminating with the language, since it is more distinctly Masonic to refer to "travel" while many other authors have deployed the metaphor of all life as a "journey," but I don't think it can do us harm to encompass both here.

When I think of literal travel, I often think of my grandparents on my mom's side, who really got to see a lot of the world in their retirement. My grandfather was the quiet, shy, and intellectual one; my grandmother was the gregarious and outgoing one. When they traveled, they would sometimes go with friends who they were already comfortable and could be at ease with; and thanks to my grandmother's outgoing nature, they were also likely to make new friends during the journey with whom they might stay in touch.

We might see our Masonic travel as being similar. As I was discussing with a friend at a meeting just the other night, as you move from one body to another you will see many familiar faces, and you will make new friends there as well. The Masonic bodies today are like a Venn diagram, with a great deal of overlap. But what are the strengths and weaknesses of trying to use that metaphor of world travel to look at the Masonic journey? I think there are three important points to consider.

First, the blend of people you encounter in a Masonic body might be viewed less as the group of people traveling with you and more like the culture of the land you are visiting.

In this case, I might actually prefer it if the mix of people included more of the new—I'd like my Scottish Rite experience to have a flavor that's distinct from my Shrine experience, and those distinct from my York Rite experience, and those distinct from my Tall Cedars experience. I would like my travels to challenge my palate and broaden my mind.

Second, if the preponderance of familiar faces means that the same individuals are taking on leadership roles in multiple organizations, this could be a red flag. Even with the best of intentions, wanting to serve their fellow members and support bodies that are in need of assistance, we run a risk of simply burning people out.

And third, if the desire to explore the many appendant bodies may be analogous to the curiosity or sense of adventure that inspires us to travel to new and different lands, we should make sure not to take for granted the treasures in our own backyard. It is possible to be worldly, but not be versed in the heritage of your native land. I know there are people who have dedicated more of their time, in a focused manner, to an ongoing study of blue lodge—traveling more in their native country instead of farther afield—and the depth of their knowledge speaks well of them.

In addition to traveling through space, we might discuss the notion of traveling through time. Is this a farfetched idea best consigned to the realm of science fiction? Yes and no. It is true that we have not yet developed a technology or method that permits us to travel backwards and forwards (or sideways!) through time in a controlled and intentional fashion. But approximating this kind of activity in thought and language is not so foreign as it might sound at first. After all, language is used in the second degree regarding all of us traveling forward in time, as we progress naturally through life. Physics suggests that time might be somewhat like a dimension in space (dimensions that we use in very common terms, such as width and height), so that in the same way as we might say, viewed from above, what is in front of us and what is behind us exists on the same level plane as where we stand presently, we might say that if we could be distanced somehow from the "plane" of time, we would see that the past and the future coexist together with the present, all in this plane of being.

If you can get comfortable with this thought exercise, perhaps we can expand in another direction. What might we mean by moving "sideways" in time? It has been suggested that if the created universe is infinite, there must exist "somewhere" a reality like ours in every detail except for one consequential decision or outcome—a "parallel" reality (a concept first proposed by a Princeton physics graduate student named Hugh Everett in 1957). The physical analogue to aid our imagination is that if we are traveling along a timeline, in the world as we know it, this parallel reality would result from a decision or outcome that differed slightly in the past, resulting in a different present "next to" us.

It might be said that by utilizing memory, we can at least figuratively travel backward in time. We might agree it is valuable to reflect on the experience of the past, to guide us in understanding the state of our present or preparing us to make better-informed choices for our future. It might also be said that in exercising our imaginations, we are capable of traveling "sideways" to examine those hypotheticals of what might have been. But I feel this is a dangerous pitfall; is it not futile to become preoccupied with what might have been, when what's done is done and we cannot alter the current state once the lot has been cast?

But I think we might benefit from the notion of traveling to the future, at least mentally. Some frameworks for describing this, such as Creative Visualization, are somewhat mystical and not very scientifically grounded suggesting that the mere act of envisioning can shape or direct the future. But many strategists will advocate picturing the desired end state in order to work toward it. Even Stephen Covey touts, "Begin with the end in mind" as the first of his "The 7 Habits of Highly Effective People." And futurist Joel Barker has presented on "The Power of Vision" to myriad organizations.

There is a phrase we deploy in the first degree, trying to explain to the candidate many curious details of his initiatic experience, asserting that all of them carry weight and significance. I believe the concept of travel as a symbol is no exception. So, whether we speak of traveling across the terrestrial orb, among the Masonic bodies, or even through time itself, I hope you will pause to appreciate the power of language and metaphor, and what it can truly mean for a Mason to be a traveling man.

Tolerance

Originally published in *RiteNow*, Vol. XXVIII, No. 4, June 2019

In this issue we turn our attention to the core values of the Scottish Rite. This very notion of the "core values" is an interesting and recent adaptation. While we may treasure the many degrees in Scottish Rite working and value them as conveying distinct lessons through individual dramatic conclusions, someone believed it would be valuable to encapsulate in more succinct fashion "what is taught" in Scottish Rite. This resulted in the distillation that is placed before us of six core values perceived as the common threads within the work. Personally, I choose to focus on the value labeled "toleration."

To begin with, we know what happens when people live side by side without the principle of toleration: categorizing someone as beneath you—fundamentally unworthy of the same consideration and esteem as yourself—is a slippery slope towards dehumanizing the other party. It is a sure recipe for disharmony, at the very least, and atrocity at the worst. We have seen it throughout history; if you read ordinary media and literature from settings such as the period of slavery in the early United States or under the Third Reich in Nazi Germany, you routinely encounter language that either implies or explicitly states that some categories of people are subhuman and therefore not entitled to proper human rights. Although we like to pat ourselves on the back and believe we have come a long way, this kind of thinking persists into the present, and we should be on the lookout for similar language.

It is easy to call to mind several of the degrees that depict the encounter between differing belief systems and how those interactions can play out. Among these I think of the 24th degree, Brother of the Forest; the 29th degree, Knight of St. Andrew; and a dear favorite of mine, the Four Chaplains degree, based on the true story of Lieutenants George Fox, Alexander Goode, John Washington, and Clark Poling. In 1943, these four chaplains of different faiths (Methodist, Jewish, Roman Catholic, and Dutch Reformed) were assigned to the US Army transport ship, the Dorchester. In the early hours of February 3, the ship was fired upon by a submarine and as the ship sank, these men not only worked together to evacuate the servicemen, but they gave away their own life vests to ensure that as many of them as possible would survive.

If we examine these degrees carefully, we come away with more than an admonition to "tolerate" the beliefs of others, which is partly why I wanted to focus on this core value. Admittedly, the person or persons who took on the labor of communicating these unifying threads within our degree work had the unenviable task of trying to capture the essence of profound wisdom in bullet points. But "tolerance" can be read with a subtly elitist undertone, implying that you "tolerate" the other belief system you have encountered, as

 MORE LIGHT

though it is a valiant act of being benevolent in your supe-riority. While some might say this is splitting hairs, I believe that language and symbolism matter quite a bit, and the notion of tolerance seems lukewarm in comparison to something more like acceptance or respect.

The degrees I call to mind above, on the other hand, suggest that if we encounter our fellow man with an open mind, we will likely be surprised to discover how much our belief systems are alike, emphasizing our commonalities rather than our dissimilarities. The Mahabharata of ancient India states "treat others as you treat yourself." "You shall love your neighbor as yourself" originates with Leviticus (Vayikra) 19:17. In Luke 6:31 Jesus is quoted as saying "do unto others as you would have them do unto you." The Quran in passage 41:34 states, ". . . Nor can goodness and Evil be equal. Repel Evil with what is better: Then will he between whom and you was hatred become as it were your friend and intimate." Kung-Fu-Tze (Confucius) said, "what you do not wish for yourself, do not do to others," and the concept is also echoed by the Greeks and the Zoroastrians.

The common ground of the world's major religions is also the province of a school of thought called theosophy, a study of the primordial truths that underpin them all when divested of their superfluities. The term "theosophy" first came into use somewhere between the third and sixth century CE among the Alexandrian Neoplatonists and found a resurgence among Meister Eckhart in the fourteenth century, Jacob Boehme in the seventeenth century, Emanuel Swedenborg in the eighteenth century, and Madame Blavatsky in the nineteenth century. Early Christian or Bochmian theosophy focuses on the pursuit of intimate personal contact with deity, which attracted some negative attention from the Catholic Church as it deemphasized the role of a party responsible for mediating that interaction. The latter outgrowth of the movement since 1875 in the West is sometimes regarded the province of esotericism. But its aims are fairly straightforward—the American Theosophical Society's mission statement is "to encourage open-minded inquiry into world religions, philosophy, science, and the arts in order to understand the wisdom of the ages, respect the unity of all life, and help people explore spiritual self-transformation." The Theosophists are still active today and, if anyone else is curious to visit the society in Pittsburgh, I should like to organize an outing.

I would be remiss if I did not mention here, that when my congregation Tree Of Life / Or L'Simcha was attacked by an individual on October 27, 2018, the Islamic Center of Pittsburgh was quick to come to our aid, organizing very successful fundraising. In the wake of the shooting at the mosque in Christchurch, New Zealand, on March 15, 2019, our congregation both reached out to that mosque and supported the Islamic Center of Pittsburgh's fundraising efforts to improve their security. We have a long history of looking out for our own—these tragedies have been a stark reminder that an assault on the religious liberties of any of us is an assault on the religious liberties of all of us. In the haunting words of the German Lutheran pastor Martin Niemoller, "First they came for the socialists, and I did not speak out—because I was not a socialist. Then they came for the trade unionists, and I did not speak out—because I was not a trade unionist. Then they came for the Jews, and I did not speak out—because I was not a Jew. Then they came for me—and there was no one left to speak for me."

In conclusion, I believe this core value of toleration deserves our attention, but that it should really be a jumping-off point. We should be willing and ready to go beyond toleration to learn about different faiths and schools of thought, so that we may respect and enrich each other, and support and defend each other. As Masons we are taught that every human being is entitled to our charitable ministrations. As Scottish Rite Masons, the lesson of toleration should lead to the lessons of acceptance and respect because these lessons are essential to our goal of worldwide brotherhood, and the creation of a fit abiding place for the Grand Architect of the Universe, in the world at large, and within ourselves.

Council of Deliberation

Originally published in *RiteNow*, Vol. XXIX, No. 1, September 2019

We may be better prepared both to enjoy the benefits of Scottish Rite Masonry in the Valley of Pittsburgh, as well as to support and serve it, the better informed we are. To that end, I would like to shed a little light on the function of our Council of Deliberation.

To set this in context, I would like to "zoom out" for a moment, to an even larger body or structure, the Northern Masonic Jurisdiction. The Northern Masonic Jurisdiction consists of the fifteen states north of the Mason-Dixon Line and east of the Mississippi. The Supreme Council governs Scottish Rite Masonry in this jurisdiction, is headquartered in Lexington MA, and is led by our Sovereign Grand Commander (as of this writing, July 2019, in the person of Illustrious David A. Glattly, 33°). The Council of Deliberation functions as an efficient state-level division to help coordinate this extensive organization.

What is the business of Council of Deliberation? According to the Pennsylvania Council of Deliberation website, it "possesses the legislative and judicial powers not reserved to the Supreme Council and not inconsistent with the Constitution and Regulations." This means it has the right to create rules governing the Scottish Rite valleys in Pennsylvania to any extent not already covered by Supreme Council, and judge the extent of compliance with those rules.

It consists of:

- The Deputy—Your state has one deputy. He is the representative of the Sovereign Grand Commander (head authority of Scottish Rite, Northern Masonic Jurisdiction) for your entire state and the emissary from Supreme Council to your state. In this way, he's kind of like a District Deputy.
- Honorary members of Supreme Council (33rd degree)—Anyone who has been unanimously elected at an annual meeting of Supreme Council to receive this recognition for their service to the Scottish Rite or in other branches of Masonry
- Active members of Supreme Council (33rd degree)—Like a board of directors, they are 33rds who have been tapped to take added responsibility for helping the Deputy regulate valleys within some geographic segment of their state. They are eligible to move up to Deputy. Every valley has only one Active 33rd assigned to represent them to the Deputy and each Active 33rd can be responsible for one or several valleys.
- Several ceremonial officers
- A master of ceremonies
- A sentinel

The body of voting members also consists of:
- The top three officers in Consistory for every valley (Commander-in-Chief, First Lieutenant Commander, Second Lieutenant Commander)
- The top three officers in Rose Croix for every valley (Most Wise Master, Senior Warden, Junior Warden)
- The top four officers in Princes of Jerusalem for every valley (Sovereign Prince, High Priest, Senior Warden, Junior Warden)
- The top four officers in Lodge of Perfection for every valley (Thrice Potent Master, Deputy Master, Senior Warden, Junior Warden)

Formally speaking, the Actives are "elected and installed" officers. For practical purposes, they are chosen by the Sovereign Grand. They can serve in their position until the first annual meeting of Supreme Council that takes place after they turn seventy-five, at which point they attain Active Emeritus status.

Throughout the Northern Masonic Jurisdiction, each state has a number of Actives based on the number of Scottish Rite members in the state. Some states have as few as two actives; Pennsylvania, with a more substantial Scottish Rite presence, has five. For the state of Pennsylvania, our actives as of this writing (July 2019) are:
- Illustrious George Nakonetschny, 33°—Valleys of Allentown, Bloomsburg, and Towanda
- Illustrious Paul J. Roup, 33°—Valleys of Altoona, Pittsburgh, and Uniontown
- Illustrious Thomas R. Labagh, 33°—Valleys of Coudersport, Harrisburg, Lancaster, and Williamsport

- Illustrious Robert J. Bateman, 33°—Valleys of Philadelphia, Reading, and Scranton
- Illustrious Keith E. Parkinson, 33°—Valleys of Erie, New Castle, and Oil City

One of the Actives from your state is your Deputy. He is personally selected by the Sovereign Grand and serves as his surrogate in any Scottish Rite business in the state, which gives him a great deal of authority and responsibility. His term limit is eight years, at which time he reverts back to Active and must be replaced as Deputy, or until he reaches seventy-five years of age, at which time he attains Emeritus status and must be replaced.

(In our case in Pennsylvania, we happen to be in a transitional phase where Illustrious Thomas K. Sturgeon, 33°, is in the process of "passing the torch" of his Deputy role to Illustrious Robert J. Bateman, 33°, and that of Active to Illustrious Paul J. Roup, 33°.)

The Council of Deliberation convenes once a year. In Pennsylvania, this is usually a weekend in mid-July. At the Council of Deliberation, several recognitions are awarded to entire valleys based on membership gains and charitable fundraising. Individual recognition is also awarded to recipients of the Meritorious Service Award. Per the Scottish Rite NMJ website, "The Meritorious Service Award may be conferred upon members of the Rite in this Jurisdiction who have attained the 32° and who, by reason of meritorious service of a Masonic character, are deemed worthy of such recognition."

Also, the current Actives bring their nominations to receive the 33rd to Council of Deliberation. They hold a private meeting on Friday to discuss which nominations will be brought to the Supreme Council executive meeting in August. Again, according to the Scottish Rite NMJ website, "A 33° Mason is a Master Mason who has exhibited knowledge, passion and sacrifice to his craft. The Supreme Council awards the 33° as a way of honoring outstanding and selfless work performed in the Rite or in public life."

Attending a session of Council of Deliberation carries at least two benefits that immediately come to mind: it impresses upon one the breadth and scope of Scottish Rite across the state and it affords wonderful opportunities for strengthening existing fellowship, as well as forging new bonds. I hope that this overview leaves you feeling better informed and equipped, and you will avail yourself of your next opportunity to attend Pennsylvania Council of Deliberation.

Light on Light

Originally published in *RiteNow*, Vol. XXIX, No. 2, December 2019

You know, I didn't title my column "More Light" for no reason. Masonry has many facets—fellowship, charity, spirituality—but among them, the learning we engage in through the exchange of ideas in forums such as this is what I prize most highly. Today it is my pleasure to examine with you the symbolism of darkness and light, and how two different perspectives "interact" with each other: light as good and darkness as evil; and light as knowledge and darkness as ignorance.

The assignment of the values, light as good and darkness as evil, must originate incredibly far back in human history and can be understood in the context of primitive life. Primitive human life was always in greatest danger during the hours of darkness from predators better adapted to seeing at night. Likewise, in a more subtle application, when it comes to organic matter, various toxic or unhealthy processes can happen in the dark such as mold or mildew; once exposed to light they can at least begin to be cleaned and disinfected. Therefore, it makes intuitive sense that humans may have begun associating good and evil with light and dark from very early on, and it would have become more codified and ritualized as societies with spiritual or religious symbolism developed.

When we talk about light as good and darkness as evil, we are very much hearkening back to primitive belief systems and may even experience awkward feelings around this. On one hand, we are not choosing to follow a model, such as the Egyptians or Greeks, and worship the sun as a god itself. On the other hand, in the Jewish tradition, the sun and the moon take on a symbolic significance for communicating our relationship to the creator; as the sun is a source of light and the moon can only reflect the light from this source, so God is the source of all good, while righteous people should reflect that "light." (I will refer more to reflection later.)

In fact, the signification of light as good and dark as evil has become so popular in cultures throughout the world as to become what I might refer to as a "symbolic blind spot"—so pervasive that we almost equate the symbol with the interpretation and forget that we are engaging in a deliberate act of association, because the connection has become so instinctive. For example, consider that a horror or suspense movie is more likely to have the bulk of the action take place at night or in the darkness, in spite of the fact that, in reality, many unfortunate horrors are perpetrated in broad daylight. Consider also the way this symbolic association has unfortunately played out in attitudes about race. When lightness is associated with good and darkness with evil, and when this choice of perspective is just assumed to be common sense, terrible and senseless inequity may proceed from it.

The other perspective or interpretation to examine, then, is light as knowledge and darkness as ignorance. It is also unsurprising that we as humans eventually arrived at this association, when you consider that 90% of the information transmitted to the brain is visual (this, supposedly supported by research from 3M Corporation). When we use this metaphor, we simply equate "not seeing" with "not knowing." This is the sense in which we use darkness as a metaphor in Masonic initiation.

How well this metaphor works depends very much on how you choose to define knowledge itself. Consider first that in Masonry we could be talking about any one of several different kinds or areas of knowledge. Is the Mason's goal to understand more about Masonry, or about himself as a man? If the former, consider the four stages of competence, first referenced by management trainer Martin Broadwell in 1969:

- Unconscious incompetence—The individual does not know how to do something, but doesn't even realize their deficiency
- Conscious incompetence—The individual realizes what the knowledge set is, out in the world, and is aware of what they don't know
- Conscious competence—The individual has learned things, is aware of what they have absorbed with effort, and can recall them with effort
- Unconscious competence—The individual is so steeped in the knowledge that they can perform their skills and tasks as second nature

If the latter, consider instead the variant that is represented by the Johari window: if you and your peers were to select adjectives that apply to you and arrange them in the categories of how I see myself, how I do not see myself, how others see me, and how others do not see me, the agreements and disagreements here could be most informative.

Drawing from the Jewish tradition, there are three categories of knowledge:

- Chokmah, which is ordinarily translated as "wisdom," which is the spontaneous, sudden flash of insight or inspiration from an "unknown" origin (the supernal realm and thence from God).
- Binah, which is ordinarily translated as "understanding," which is deductive reasoning, understanding one idea from another.
- Da'at, which is ordinarily translated as "knowledge," which is associated with the powers of memory and concentration, but also, intimate, as derived from personal experience (and therefore the root of the biblical euphemism "to know").

Given what we consider the source, if any of these types of knowledge should be symbolized by the light, I would be inclined to say it is Chokmah.

I think an interesting further examination of the metaphor of light and darkness is a modern view of light as radiation or signal. One might imagine, then, that a person, an ethical actor who is exposed to the light, is within range and receiving signal from the source of all good; if the signal is blocked or interfered with, the ethical actor is effectively in a shadow, in a dead zone, receiving no signal; likewise, one might be capable of acting as a repeater or a reflector in this metaphysical system, helping bring the signal into a region previously cast in shadow.

This takes me one step further to a place where the metaphor can fail us, and the reason why I think our definition of knowledge is very important to the discussion. If light symbolizes "knowledge" but also "good," then why would intelligent people ever do evil things? And yet we know, by a generally accepted definition of intelligence, that intelligent people are perfectly capable of doing evil, and do so. It could be that in our Masonic ritual, we have one tiny modifier—one simple adjective, maybe frequently ignored and overlooked, but perhaps intended to specify for us what type of knowledge must be pursued in our journey from darkness to true Masonic light.

The Elephant (and Donkey) in the Room

Originally published in *RiteNow*, Vol. XXIX, No. 4, June 2020

Knowing that the theme of the upcoming issue was the Masonic value of patriotism and love of country, the temptation I faced to write a puff piece was strong. Nothing could be simpler than to espouse the things about our country that I do love, and then to have our brethren read it, nodding sagely, agreeing that "good is good," and then try to scurry as quickly as possible to the next thing. But as much as I cringed at the prospect, I felt that as adults we ought to acknowledge the fractious political climate in our country and attempt to address it, as civilized gentlemen, as brothers.

Many of you who are interested in history will already know two things about party politics in America. First, most of the founding fathers warned against it. James Madison wrote in *The Federalist Papers* that one of the goals of a "well-constructed union" ought to be "its tendency to break and control the violence of faction." Alexander Hamilton once referred to political parties as "the most fatal disease" of a government by the people.

Second, Americans began engaging in party politics anyway, and very early. The Democratic Party's basic roots began in 1791, and their chief opposition, the Whigs, coalesced in opposition to President (and brother) Andrew Jackson in 1834, to spin off later into the Republican Party in 1854. Incidentally, in this period from the 1790s to the 1810s, newspapers were very explicit tools of the parties, and if you think today's political coverage is vicious, you really ought to try reading the old stuff some time.

All of this is why (if you'll forgive me skipping around in time) George Washington famously warned in his farewell speech in 1796 of the deleterious effects of parties on our democracy: "The common and continual mischiefs of the spirit of party are sufficient to make it the interest and duty of a wise people to discourage and restrain it."

Entangled with our perception of our contemporary Democratic and Republican parties is our understanding of what it means to be "liberal" or "conservative":

One definition of "liberal" *might* be the stance that the government's role is to serve and protect the public, and that in doing so, it needs to pay particular attention to segments of the population that are most disadvantaged and vulnerable; that to preserve liberty and equality for those who are powerless or at-risk may involve putting safety nets in place for them, possibly to the extent of redistribution of wealth.

One definition of "conservative" *might* be the stance expressed in the maxim "that government is best which governs least" (often misattributed to Jefferson and best remembered as a quote in Henry David Thoreau's *Civil Disobedience*, who was quoting the motto of *The United States Magazine and Democratic Review*). This is to say that if I am going to consent to be governed, please govern me as efficiently as possible by being frugal and efficient with the tax money you extract from me and interfere with my freedoms as little as possible.

I can say without irony or pandering that I can find something to admire in both stances. Please reread both passages carefully and with an open mind. Can you not say the same?

It's worth including in this discussion that America has had, and still has, "third parties" aside from the Democrats and Republicans. A quick trip to Wikipedia seeking "political parties in the United States" can introduce you to the Constitution Party, the Green Party, and the Libertarian Party; but this is just constraining it to the larger and more broadly-recognized ones. If you continue down the rabbit hole to the "list of political parties in the United States," you'll find a total of forty or so. Some are strictly regional and only operate in a state or two. Others are a bit one-note, or seem to have only one "plank" in their platform. But a conclusion we can easily draw is that there are ideologies further left and further right than those espoused by our mainstream political parties.

And it's also okay to bring into this discussion the perennial debate between "voting your conscience" versus "doing the math." If you've ever been disillusioned with the plans and actions of both major parties and contemplated aloud supporting one of these other alternatives, you will almost inevitably encounter friends who want to warn you that voting your conscience accomplishes nothing; it only erodes the pursuit of the needed majority by one of the mainstream candidates. I must confess, in our current system, I know that desire looks pretty Quixotic.

Where do we go from here? If we look to our Scottish Rite teaching, there is indeed some guidance. As usual, I will do my best to allude to it here without capturing anything inappropriate in print. You should find nothing more revealing in what I write than what appears at our Scottish Rite NMJ website: in the 20th degree, set during the Revolutionary War, Masons are able to agree upon a judgment regarding right and wrong, and even with an active and serious issue dividing them at the time, they can come to this accord; and in the 26th degree, set during the Civil War, Masons are willing to offer comfort and succor to each other in spite of their divisions.

In addition to those two more obvious examples, though, I would like to add the following, which I would deem a very important example, if the audience will forgive my possible bias: in the 16th degree, we witness a debate in the court of King Darius. Three participants propose arguments which—you will only learn with further study—benefit them because of their relationships to the king. Only one man makes his argument, not because of a connection to power and influence or how it will benefit him, but based on what is right and true. I'll acknowledge that this lesson can be the trickiest to apply because in our zeal, we often believe that we are possessed of the only objective truth. We must proceed with caution.

With this said, I think it's time we turn a serious and critical eye on our own public conduct. And yes, I know none of us have been much in public as a result of the virus-related lockdown. But I'm referring to our conduct on the internet: that Agora which never closes, a venue where we were sharing our thoughts and opinions before this quarantine, have done even more so during, and will no doubt continue after. I can scarcely believe this needs to be repeated, but how we conduct ourselves in public is a demonstration to non-members and could be their only window into what Freemasonry is about. Ad hominem attacks, name-calling, and broad sweeping generalizations about the supporters of one party or another should be rigorously avoided—it's immature and suggests there is nothing lofty about our association. Remember, every time you say "all (X) are nincompoops" or wish some terrible fate upon their ilk, you are likely including in that statement someone whom you bear no personal ill will, and would otherwise wish them health, happiness, and success.

Is it possible that we can all agree that internal forces are contributing to the erosion of our democracy? Maybe you consider the great evil is campaign finance or the infusion of "dark money" into American politics; maybe you think the greatest issue is the monolithic nature of the mainstream parties; maybe you think it's the replacement of debate over candidates' qualifications with identity politics and pandering. But we as brothers ought to step up, acknowledge these divisions, and be the vanguard of seeking the common ground. This could be our greatest act of patriotism in our lifetimes.

Living in the Chamber of Reflection

Originally published in *RiteNow*, Vol. XXX, No. 1, September 2020

In 2019, I experienced the loss of several loved ones hitting closer and closer to home. It began with a dear blue lodge brother and the father of my first-line signer, Jay Cohen, who passed away on February 3; then my aunt, Francine Shifrin, passed away May 6; my stepfather, Marvin Sweet, passed away September 1; and my grandmother, Gladyce Novick, passed away on October 13.

In 2020, the world has been subject to illness and death more broadly than we have seen in a century as a result of the virus outbreak, and while we try in varying ways to soldier on, our own mortality may often be on our minds.

When I think of my own mortality my thoughts often wander to the Chamber of Reflection. The Chamber of Reflection is a small room containing symbols of mortality, which was once used as part of Masonic initiation. The candidate was to spend some time there contemplating these symbols prior to undergoing the ceremony, for as the author Johann Christian Gadicke said, "It is only in solitude that we can deeply reflect upon our present or future undertakings, and blackness, darkness, or solitariness is ever a symbol of death. A man who has undertaken a thing after mature reflection seldom turns back."

Among several symbols employed in this room, one usually finds a banner with the acronym V.I.T.R.I.O.L., representing the Latin phrase, *Visita Interiora Terrae, Rectificandoque, Invenies Occultum Lapidem*, which translates approximately as "visit the interior of the earth, and purifying it, you will find the hidden stone." (This comes to us by way of the Rosicrucians and the *tabula smaragdina*, or emerald tablet, in case you wish to do some supplementary research.) While it's more tantalizing to suppose this is a reference to the philosopher's stone of alchemical lore, a more practical, psychological interpretation is that it enjoins us to look within ourselves for hidden answers we seek.

Reflecting on mortality can serve just such productive and positive purposes. We are taught in lodge rhetoric that we should view our mortality as a great equalizer, a part or reminder of the common human bond. In addition to that lesson, I'd posit that this contemplation should also stimulate us to treat our unknown remaining balance of time on Earth as precious and put it to good use, cherish our affiliations while we may enjoy them, and let our loved ones know that they are loved.

Death itself figures into several of our Masonic allegories. Of course, I will avoid putting into print anything which I ought not to. Suffice it to say, if you can think of any of the degree work to which I'm alluding, you might ask yourself, what would you genuinely be willing to lay down your life for? It's one thing to say that you have memorized lessons that convey some moral conclusion—that you know the code or the tenets—but have you ever truly tried to picture a scenario where you would be ready to make "the ultimate sacrifice," and how confident are you that you know how you'd behave?

Death also comes up in a slogan or credo which appears in both the York Rite and Scottish Rite: *Virtus Junxit, Mors Non Separabit* or "what virtue has joined, let death not put asunder." This can be applied in a few somewhat different contexts but is generally taken to represent our wish that what the force of good has united through the actions of Freemasonry should outlast death.

Is this naïve optimism? I think we will acknowledge that death separates us from our friends and loved ones, apart from the extent to which we may feel comfort from "speaking with them" even beyond those events. But I also think it is reasonable to say that from one perspective, that which Masonry sets in motion truly does outlast death, summarized aptly by brother Albert Pike when he said, "What we do for ourselves dies with us. What we do for others and the world remains and is immortal." Freemasonry, among several tenets, attempts to teach us to extend charity (not just of material means but charity of spirit) toward our brother, and to gradually extend that charity to all humankind. If we can live up to this, then surely its impact, the echoes, domino effect, or what have you, will indeed outlast our own lifetime.

Of course, there is, without question, a risk that our contemplation of mortality, instead of leading us down a path of reasoning that inspires us to take what time we have and make the most of it, could take a dark and morbid turn. If we are convinced that the fleeting and unpredictable nature of human life makes our labors futile, it's hard to maintain hope in the face of that conclusion.

This is the challenge we face. We have entered this chamber and been confronted with our own mortality, and it is possible that, as with initiation, some great transformation awaits us when we emerge and that our next step takes us to the threshold of a new way of living. But our wait here in the chamber of reflection has grown to feel like an interminable purgatory, with no way of knowing how long we have left to go. Thankfully, one flaw in this analogy is that we are not in the chamber alone. Even as we try to maintain some safe social distance, at least we know we are all undergoing this trial together. If we bear this in mind, that even in these strange and isolating times we are truly not alone, then hopefully we can support each other even though this test, sharing our hopes and fears around what has already passed and what lies ahead, until we emerge from *Interiora Terrae* to the light of a new day.

Where Two or Three are Gathered Together

Originally published in *RiteNow*, Vol. XXX, No. 2, December 2020

The global pandemic has disrupted so much in 2020 that I don't think we can discuss any topic without being forced to address how the virus has impacted it as well. When it comes to religion and spirituality, that impact has been at the forefront of my mind recently—how compliance with the recommendation not to gather in large groups indoors impacts people's observance and practice of their faith.

Stepping back for a moment, I understand there are some very subjective variables here. I understand some people's practice has always involved more solitude and introspection—a monastic practice, for instance. And I can see a very sound line of reasoning there: if your experience of the Divine in the world is "the still, small voice," then you need that quiet and stillness to commune with the Divine; and maybe that communion is not only possible, but even best achieved, without the company of other people.

I would be interested to hear from people whose practice falls within that school and learn more about whether this time in our history has had an impact on their observance that I wouldn't even have thought of. Now, with that said about what others' experiences might be like, here is a much more personal take:

When the lockdown began, my congregation stopped holding Saturday morning services for the Sabbath. There were Friday evening services, held over Zoom, but Friday nights had never been my preference even when we were still able to meet in person; the prayers and melodies are different and it's just not my favorite. But now this was my only choice because according to Jewish prohibitions during the Sabbath, you can operate electronics, tools, and devices such as your computer on Friday before sundown, as the Sabbath hasn't started yet, but you can't on Saturday morning while it's in effect.

Now I haven't had a perfect attendance record in some time. I was once the guy who was there three or four weeks out of the month, and later became a guy who was there one or two weeks out of the month. That's a familiar trend for a lot of people. But now having no choice in the matter made me uneasy. I missed greeting people. I missed singing the prayers together. I missed the little luncheon and the kibitzing after services. I missed that feeling of community.

It's worth noting here that this didn't mean I couldn't find other expressions for my connection to God. I have my own custom of saying grace before meals, for instance. It feels appropriate, that routine expression of gratitude, so I was able to "keep the fire burning" in my own small way.

But as the High Holy Days (Rosh Hashanah, the new year, and Yom Kippur, the Day of Atonement) grew closer this year, I was concerned and anxious. These are among a few holidays in our religious calendar when it's considered imperative that everyone in the community assemble in the temple. What were we going to do under the circumstances? When the word came out that services were going to be held over Zoom, I felt a bizarre combination of relieved, quizzical, and skeptical all at once.

When the experience finally arrived, it brought me great happiness. Yes, it had many of the quirks that some of us have already experienced using telecommunications like this for work—occasional lag, confusion about the mute button, the small surprising window into other people's home environs, even a few cute pets. But more importantly, it felt really good. I welled up a bit when I saw all these familiar faces within their tiny squares on my monitor. I was so glad to hear from our Rabbi and sing these ancient melodies "together" again, and even with the weird distortion, hear the sound of the shofar over Zoom.

When an act of domestic terrorism was committed in my synagogue, Tree of Life / Or L'Simcha, on October 27, 2018— when we lost eleven of our brothers and sisters—we were also displaced from our house of worship in a modern diaspora which continues as of this writing. The actions of the gunman as well as some of the maneuvers required to arrest him, left the building very badly damaged. We have since convened in several other locations, among them, the Katz Theater of the JCC, Rodef Shalom in Oakland, Beth Shalom in Squirrel Hill, and Calvary Episcopal Church in Shadyside.

In the wake of the event, many of us longed for the day we could return to our building. Especially for those whose families belonged to Tree of Life before two congregations merged and had a long history there, the prospect of that symbolic homecoming became very important. But at the same time, as we mourned and healed together, another notion became salient as well; the meaning and importance of the building is a separate consideration from the importance of the community.

If you've ever used Zoom, or any one of several other video-conferencing applications, for work or personal use, you are already familiar with some of the quirks of the experience I have described; and if you use any of them enough, you too may have experienced a feeling I think I'm starting to adapt to, which is the illusion of shared presence. I have been in remote work meetings, when a manager has taken roll and very naturally used the same language that we would if we were gathered in person somewhere, "Is so-and-so here?" But where is the "here" he is speaking of? It's the imagined or virtual shared space "wherever we are." It takes me back to things the science fiction author William Gibson posited about cyberspace back when I was a kid, before cyberspace existed.

As I said, I was quite hesitant and skeptical at the prospect of conducting religious services in this weird and ethereal medium; but in the absence of any other safe option, I found the experience an acceptable if not-totally-satisfying substitute. If your cultural take on religious or spiritual experience has a communal component, could virtual telepresence ever supply that aspect? Could it do so for our Masonic experience?

If we think about making the best possible use of the tools at our disposal, to deliver the best possible experience for brethren, we must assess the strengths and weaknesses of the tools and the qualities we want the experience to have. We may have been forced into exploring telepresence by circumstances of health and safety, but now that we find ourselves at this stage, we might also contemplate whether further evolution of the tools, and improvement upon their functionality, could result in us seeing them in a more favorable light, and deploying them for even more purposes. Back in 2014, I wrote an article for *Rite News* (the former name of the magazine *RiteNow*) on the past, present, and future of Scottish Rite Ritual which included this passage:

> *The more I have thought about it, I gradually came to wonder if my instinct to preserve ritual in its live-performance form is overly conservative or reactionary. Earlier, I may have been emphasizing the difference between entertainment and education, but there is something they have in common: Much like the entertainment options available to the public have changed and expanded as a result of modern technology, so too have educational tools: consider the current popularity of internet-based classes, or Massive Open Online Courses; think of the way the military and emergency responders make use of simulation technology for training.*

Thinking back on this flight of fancy I had, but in the context of all the virtual gatherings of the last seven months, it came to me in kind of a flash: a whole different interpretation of the "house not made with hands;" not exactly in the heavens but a placeless place that we are taking tiny steps toward creating, a new and different kind of place where two or three can still gather together in God's name, and He will be in the midst of them.

Integrity: A Linguistic and Symbolic Exploration

Originally published in *RiteNow*, Vol. XXX, No. 3, March 2021

When I began contemplating what I want to say to you about integrity, it took me on quite a flight of fancy, and I hope I'll be able to pull it together in some fashion that will be gratifying for the reader.

In blue lodge Masonry, I have lectured before about the interesting feature of English vocabulary concerning morals and ethics, and how much of it seems to derive from geometric or architectural metaphor, such as describing a person as "upright" or "crooked," asking someone to be honest with you in terms of whether the person or their story is "on the level," or referring to a fair transaction as a "square deal." This is not meant to suggest that English owes this symbolic vocabulary to Freemasonry, but at the very least we can safely say the symbolism is deeply embedded in our language. It did not occur to me until today that "integrity" also falls into this category.

In Freemasonry we retell the story of the construction of the great temple in Israel by King Solomon, Hiram King of

Tyre, Hiram Abiff, and a veritable army of workmen. At its conclusion we remark on how beautiful the finished product was, owing to its expertly planned, managed, and executed assembly. When we speak of the integrity of a structure, much as when we speak of the integrity of a prepared dish such as a soufflé, we are using some aspects of the word—"the state of being whole, entire, or undiminished; a sound, unimpaired, or perfect condition"—which, to my thinking, inform the other fashion in which we also use the word—"adherence to moral and ethical principles; soundness of moral character; honesty."

The word "sound," used as part of that first definition, is also either synonymous with or used interchangeably with the word "sane." They both carry implications of health, even if we tend to apply one word more typically to physical health and one more typically to mental health. Many of us are familiar from the reading of a will, with that phrase regarding "being of sound mind and body." And why is it important that the person writing the will be of sound mind? In this example, the writer states this to dispel any doubts about their statements that will follow, regarding their choices for disposition of their assets.

In legal systems that are probably most familiar to me and this audience we do not hold the person who is not of sound mind responsible for their actions. So, in cases where people are accused of criminal acts, we also want to determine whether the actor was of sound mind at the time as a component of whether they will be judged innocent or guilty. I know this has raised some debate as to whether this leads to a certain risk—do we deem the actor not guilty by reason of insanity, while the very reason we deem the actor insane is due to their choice not to conform to societal norms, exemplified by the act of which they are accused? We are right to be concerned with this paradox and there may be no simple solution to it; it could be the subject of its own essay.

But I think when we use integrity to speak of "adherence to moral and ethical principles," there is also a somewhat subjective component to it: what moral and ethical principles are those? Those of the actor? Those of the surrounding society? What if there is some disjoint between these codes? If the adherence we speak of can be conceived of as an issue of being consistent with one's own moral code, then it makes me think a bit about role-play.

My reader may be more or less familiar with role-playing games. For someone unfamiliar with that pastime, one can imagine the idea of a fictional character that has been created by an author, and then an improvised story that subsequently takes place, utilizing the already-created character. The person playing the role can be judged on the quality of their portrayal using a metric of whether they are being "true to" the way the character was originally written. In the case of a game where players embody these fictional characters, the character creation will also usually involve deciding an ethos for your character. Is he or she good or evil? Do they prefer order (lawfulness) or chaos? And I posit that the definition of soundness or sanity that we are exploring, which has interplay with the legalistic definition of sanity as well as the definition of integrity, is this—are you playing the role of "Yourself" faithfully to the way it was originally written? I am willing to argue that I might deem a person to have "integrity" even if the code to which they display consistent adherence isn't one with which I agree 100%. (If you wish to explore this subject further, I recommend the webpage easydamus.com/alignment by the user, Realchaos, for an academic and nuanced look at this topic.)

For more insight into creating integrity, I think we can look back to our example of the integrity of a building (or indeed, even the example of the soufflé). I think it is informative to reflect that the integrity of the end-product is dependent on several inputs: the plan envisioning the outcomes before the effort is even begun, the materials used in its constitution, the tools employed in its assembly, and the skill and effort with which the component parts are brought together.

So, we might examine the following questions together:
- When you were a child, was there a roadmap laid out for your ethical development? Did your parents have plans for a religious upbringing for you from an early age? Or were other manners of ethical instruction planned in advance for you?
- When your character was originally being composed, what were the materials used in its composition? These materials were ethical lessons, ideals, and archetypes. (In this extended metaphor it is challenging to distinguish materials from tools—the ideas from the means used to convey them—but I believe it is worth keeping them distinct.)
- How were these ideals conveyed to you? These were the tools that manifested the process. Maybe by instruction, in that you were exposed to stories with morals, both factual and fictional, that were intended to influence

your development; maybe by experience, in that events that you lived through and witnessed would no doubt also shape your understanding of life choices and their consequences. Did you learn from people by the example they set? Were you exposed to Grimm's fairytales, Aesop's fables, stories of the Greek gods, the works of Shakespeare, Walt Disney? Any or all of these played a role.

- Who were the craftsmen who contributed to your formation? Parents, teachers, other relatives, peers? Other agents of the media and pop culture? All these actors had varying skillscts, motivations, and ultimate effectiveness in their parts in the undertaking.

It is worth noting that these questions need not be posed in the past tense, as we are all works in progress; but that the integrity of each layer of masonry as the building is raised is dependent upon the integrity of the layer beneath it. How much more challenging is it to remediate the tilting edifice if we did not begin with a foundation that was plum, level, and square?

I hope you enjoyed coming with me on this journey of philosophy, language, and introspection; that it will inspire you to contemplate and be mindful of your own integrity; and that it may motivate you to seek out how we, as builders, can contribute to the integrity of the world around us.

To Teach is to Learn

Originally published in *RiteNow*, Vol. XXX, No. 4, June 2021

One aspect of the Masonic lifestyle I enjoy a great deal is teaching and learning ritual. I know that most members wouldn't regard memorizing ritual as a primary objective of Freemasonry. Our fraternity presents itself as being an avenue for self-improvement, "taking good men and making them better." In pursuit of this goal, admittedly a noble one, ritual is sometimes looked upon as something of a necessary evil.

If we consider the monologues delivered by officers presiding over meetings, they frequently consist of directives regarding what kind of behavior to engage in and what kind of behavior to avoid. This can be traced as far back as the "Old Charges," such as the Regius Poem. It seems very reasonable for us to imagine the ancient trade guild from which we derive, and its custodians wishing to avoid the conduct of any member to reflect poorly on the institution. So, it can certainly be said that our elected leaders are always engaged in the activity of instructing, or teaching, our membership. And this activity takes place during prescribed segments of every stated meeting and every initiation in each blue lodge and every appendant body.

But it can also be said that there is another form of teaching that is also part of each blue lodge and every appendant body, which I would argue must be very important indeed, because we devote an enormous amount of time and mental energy to it: the task of memorizing ritual.

Some may look upon memorizing ritual as more superficial and less important than other commitments we could pledge ourselves to in order to strive to be good men and Masons. And I would consent that if one manages to memorize ritual verbatim and cannot be bothered to show kindness to his fellow man or try to make the world a better place, then it is certainly a hollow accomplishment. But I think that it should not be overlooked that engaging in the endeavors of teaching and learning ritual also contribute to our spiritual development.

Learning ritual is a humbling experience. Every time we take a new role or try to contribute these efforts to a new body, we are reminded what it means to be a beginner. We are reminded of the importance of being able to ask for help. We must be resilient enough to not be discouraged by our failures. We must be disciplined enough to carve out the time to practice, whether with our teacher or on our own, because only truly putting in the work is going to bear results.

Learning and teaching ritual is a tremendous bonding experience. Most of us who have participated in either side of that exchange have fond memories of a mentor who took us under their wing and generously gave of their time or the pride you experience as a teacher when your pupil succeeds, and you vicariously share in their triumph.

Learning ritual can be an enjoyable communal experience. I remember fondly when I joined my blue lodge there were several of us trying to learn our first degree oath at the same time, and there was a friendly competitiveness to our efforts that resulted in great camaraderie.

Teaching is an ideal channel for fulfilling the Masonic mission to try to make the world a better place, as well as pursuing an individual's hope of having that impact outlast our mortal lifetime. A favorite quote of mine from the Masonic author, Albert Pike, states, "What we do for ourselves dies with us. What we do for others and the world remains and is immortal." I have heard a similar or related sentiment, expressed in other ways. The Canadian author Wesley Henderson tells us in a family history published in 1986 that his father, Nelson, told him on his graduation day, "The true meaning of life, Wesley, is to plant trees under whose shade you do not expect to sit." He may have gotten this from David Elton Trueblood, a Quaker author, who wrote something similar in 1955 or the Indian poet, Rabindranath Tagore, who passed away in 1941, but a similar notion dates all the way back to Caecilius Statius as quoted by Cicero in his work "On Old Age" in 44 BC. And we are also aware that our predecessors, the operative Masons who worked in stone, would sometimes begin work on a cathedral whose completion they themselves would never see. What more enduring legacy can you have than to step into the chain of heritage that results when you touch someone's life with valuable instruction who may also go on to influence others? Who can foresee how far your impact may go?

Learning to be an effective teacher is a fascinating exercise as well, through which you can explore and learn quite a bit about yourself. What method or approach worked well for me as a student? Can I deploy that to help others? And for pupils who need something different, am I flexible enough to understand and adapt to their needs? What style of communication is going to be most effective to convey instruction? And, beyond being focused on my ability to express, am I a good enough listener to recognize what my pupil needs?

And it can also certainly be said that you enhance your own understanding of the subject matter through the effort of teaching others. In the course of learning ritual, I had it pointed out to me that certain order or word choice had subtle but valuable significance that I have enjoyed passing on to others as I teach, but I have also been given the opportunity to see the ritual through "new eyes," and even had things brought to my attention that I hadn't observed myself even in fifteen years of my own experience.

If you haven't yet made it part of your Masonic journey, I encourage you to become a teacher as well as a lifelong student, not only because the fraternity itself benefits and is sustained by your efforts to preserve and perpetuate our ritual, but because of what you get back in exchange. Taking on these roles in tandem will enhance your own experience and that of others; and it will deepen and strengthen your bond with your brethren.

My Friend and Guide

Originally published in *RiteNow*, Vol. XXXI, No. 1, September 2021

One of my Masonic heroes is Eric Krauss Cohen, 33°. Eric was many things to many people—he was the owner of the Carson Street Deli; he was a rock musician; he was an academic and an amateur philosopher; and over time, he was an experienced and accomplished Mason (with such attainments as serving as a warrant member of Lodge Ad Lucem No. 812 in 2007, as Worshipful Master of Tyrian Lodge No. 644 in 2009, and as Sovereign Prince in the Scottish Rite Valley of Pittsburgh in 2012–2013). Eric was my recommender and first-line signer in blue lodge and several appendant bodies. We traveled to many meetings and events together over the years. I think I can say he was my best friend, but that isn't really grounds for calling someone a "hero." The reason I say he was my hero is because of some of his admirable qualities and the valuable lessons I learned from him.

He was intellectually voracious. Eric was an avid reader and read extensively on Masonic topics as well as history, literature, psychology, and philosophy. He sought out and joined several appendant bodies, not only because he felt they needed new members in order to be preserved and sustained, but also because he was genuinely enthusiastic and eager about experiencing new ritual and learning new lessons. He was a well-traveled man in every sense of the word and enjoyed sharing stories with our friends about his colorful life before and outside of Freemasonry; and I think one of the great merits of this life experience was what a well-rounded and empathetic person it made him.

He was a stalwart supporter of our blue lodge. Eric could be counted on to take his accustomed spot on the side-lines at our stated meetings or fill in an officer's chair as needed during a degree night. He was a patient and insight-ful instructor when he taught me my oath, even making it fun despite being challenging. He wasn't like some fellows you might know, who get "seduced" by fun and fellowship in some appendant bodies, or more mystique and ritual in others, who you never see in blue lodge again. He always recognized that blue lodge is fundamental, respected its importance, and demonstrated his sincerity by showing up.

He dedicated time and energy to his creative outlet. It may not be everybody's lot to be a songwriter or musician, but it was one of several things that Eric and I had in common. However, by the time he and I met, I already thought of that as a closed chapter in my life, while Eric continued to make time for creativity in spite of being an already busy person with many other pursuits. I think that outlet was a boon to him and contributed to his mental and emotional health. When we "exercise our creative muscle," we strive to understand our own internal life better and to find new and innovative ways to express that inner life and share it with others. If you can get past the fear and discomfort that comes with being a novice at anything, I think you'll find that trying your hand as a creator in any medium has profound rewards.

He taught me something about charity. In his life, Eric faced some career setbacks that frustrated him greatly, so it was not always within his means to support the many charitable causes that Freemasonry exposes us to, to the extent that he might have liked. But he gave very selflessly of his time and energy, particularly as the chair of the walkathon in support of the dyslexia center. And this was a powerful lesson to me because seeing the example he set made me aware of something I had overlooked; on the one hand, donations are vital and much of what we wish to accomplish in fraternal charity cannot be accomplished without financial support; on the other hand, donating can sometimes be "the easy way out," a simpler means of assuaging one's own conscience while giving of one's time and energy is something that can be even more precious.

When Eric passed away in 2018, it hit all of us hard and in varying, unique ways. I didn't process it well and had a difficult time expressing to others how I felt—even people who I knew care very much about me. But one thing was fairly clear to me, and I didn't have any difficulty articulating it to others: the only fitting tribute I could pay to a man who had left such a profound impact on my life was to do my best to emulate his example and try as best I can to be of some service to others. I wish you the good fortune to encounter someone as you travel through life—within the fraternity or outside of it—that inspires you to live up to all the potential you possess, a true hero.

Beyond Toleration

Originally published in *RiteNow*, Vol. XXXI, No. 3, Winter 2022

I have spent a great deal of time contemplating the Scottish Rite principle of toleration. To some in this audience it might feel unnecessary to be reminded that I am a Jewish person. While most of my interactions within Freemasonry have only ever made me feel safe and respected, Jewish people are still vilified by some in the world at large, and the danger inherent in this has been all too brutally evidenced in recent memory. Unless you have ever experienced it, even just in the short-term, it's difficult for me to convey to you what it is like to be a minority and to rarely have your cultural position be the default setting in day-to-day society. The principle of toleration is indeed a key component of my Masonic experience, but the term itself can be construed as carrying a negative or cynical connotation that sets the bar fairly low for our treatment of those different from ourselves. That is to say that one can choose to read "toleration" in the most lukewarm fashion, that I deign to put up with those who are different than me.

With all this said, I think that together we should turn our attention to the interplay of religion and Freemasonry, even in spite of our reflex to shy away from this topic that is sometimes implied to be taboo within our organization. We are told that a monotheist may be qualified to join, a man who believes in a supreme being. While other requirements of character are outlined, the definition of his religion is not constrained any further than this. So our institution systemically respects religions as coequal. Now we wade into potentially controversial territory. If, for instance, a devout practitioner of religion X asks us whether Freemasonry is pro- or anti-X, the true and honest response is going to depend on the querent's definition of what is *sufficiently* pro-X. Following this line of reasoning, if I think that the only way to be a proper practitioner of my religion requires that I find it superior to all others, the One True Religion, then Freemasonry could be perceived to take a stance opposed to my religious beliefs.

We know some of the touchy subjects where people have felt obliged to mount a defense of the fraternity. It is not, itself, a religion and does not purport to take the place of a member's religion. If anything, it encourages him to be an enthusiastic practitioner of his own religion and to find suitable ways to express his own belief. So, what can we do with this notion that Freemasonry respects various religions as coequal? I will start right off the bat by saying that we may have to accept that it's simply incompatible with fundamentalism or zealotry. What it *is* compatible with, on the other hand, is a worldview that emphasizes the confluence of the principles underlying world religions. Let's examine that further:

In Mackey's *Encyclopedia of Freemasonry*, there is an interesting entry under the header "Religion of Freemasonry." At one point, he references Webster's four definitions of the word. The first three speak in more abstract terms about belief in God, an effort to perform the duties owed to God and our fellow man, and the distinction between religion, theology, virtue, and morality. In the fourth definition, he touches on the practice of explicitly labeling the religions belonging to different cultures and nations. He explains that given the wording of the first three definitions, Freemasonry can at least be referred to as a "religious institution," if not specifically a religion. From here, then, he proceeds to the crux of the issue:

> . . .it must be confessed that the fourth defini-
> tion does not appear to be strictly applicable
> to Masonry. It has no pretension to assume
> a place among the religions of the world as a
> sectarian 'system of faith and worship,' in the
> sense in which we distinguish Christianity
> from Judaism, or Judaism from Mohammedan-
> ism. . . It does not meddle with sectarian creeds
> or doctrines, but teaches fundamental religious
> truth. . .

Ergo, suggesting a truth that underpins or transcends all religions. To be overly simplistic, we might reference the golden rule, "Do unto others as you would have them do unto you." Not only is this notion *not* exclusively a maxim of Christianity, it even predates Christianity, as in this story from the Babylonian Talmud:

> *Once, a gentile approached the Rabbi Shammai*
> *and said that he would like to be converted to*

> *Judaism on the condition that the Rabbi could teach him everything he needed to know in the duration of time that the pupil could balance on one foot. Shammai sent him away. The gentile next approached Rabbi Hillel with the same challenge. Hillel said, "That which is despicable to you, do not do to your fellow, this is the whole Torah, and the rest is commentary, go and learn it."*

But there are more sophisticated references to what the universal truth might be. The introduction to the Kybalion states,

> *The student of Comparative Religions will be able to perceive the influence of the Hermetic Teachings in every religion worthy of the name, now known to man, whether it be a dead religion or one in full vigor in our own times. There is always a certain correspondence in spite of the contradictory features, and the Hermetic Teachings act as the Great Reconciler.*

As far as observers of comparative religion go, few have had the sheer opportunity for study and conversation on the subject to compare to the Dalai Lama, who states his position as follows:

> *I maintain that every major religion of the world – Buddhism, Christianity, Confucianism, Hinduism, Islam, Jainism, Judaism, Sikhism, Taoism, Zoroastrianism – has similar ideals of love,*

the same goal of benefiting humanity through spiritual practice, and the same effect of making their followers into better human beings. All religions teach moral precepts for perfecting the functions of mind, body, and speech. All teach us not to steal or take others' lives, and so on.

All religions agree upon the necessity to control the undisciplined mind that harbours selfishness and other roots of trouble, and each teaches a path leading to a spiritual state that is peaceful, disciplined, ethical, and wise. It is in this sense that I believe all religions have essentially the same message. Differences of dogma may be ascribed to differences of time and circumstance as well as cultural influences; indeed, there is no end to scholastic argument when we consider the purely metaphysical side of religion. However, it is much more beneficial to try to implement in daily life the shared precepts for goodness taught by all religions rather than to argue about minor differences in approach.

A Human Approach to World Peace, by His Holiness Tenzin Gyatso, the fourteenth Dalai Lama (Wisdom Publications, 1984)

In an excerpt from one of his other books, *Toward a True Kinship of Faiths: How the World's Religions Can Come Together,* he encapsulates his conclusion succinctly:

It is my fundamental conviction that compassion—the natural capacity of the human heart to feel concern for and connection with another being—constitutes a basic aspect of our nature shared by all human beings, as well as being the foundation of our happiness.

One of the most significant schools of thought on the confluence of spiritual teachings is the Theosophists. I will not deprive the reader of their right (nor absolve them of their responsibility) to look into this further themselves, but will only tease you with this selection from the introduction to *The Secret Doctrine*, by Helena Blavatsky:

It is perhaps desirable to state unequivocally that the teachings, however fragmentary and incomplete, contained in these volumes belong neither to the Hindu, the Zoroastrian, the Chaldean, nor the Egyptian religion, neither to Buddhism, Islam, Judaism nor Christianity exclusively. The Secret Doctrine is the essence of all these. Sprung from it in their origins, the various religious schemes are now made to merge back into their original element, out of which every mystery and dogma has grown, developed, and become materialized.

And does something so mystical really have a place in our fraternity, which at times can seem so practical and grounded? Consider the words of renowned author Manly P. Hall, 33°, and note well how it echoes the sentiment expressed by the Dalai Lama:

Freemasonry is not a material thing: It is a science of the soul; it is not a creed or doctrine but a universal expression of the divine wisdom. . . only those who see in it a cosmic study, a life work, a divine inspiration to better thinking, better feeling, and better living, with the spiritual attainment of enlightenment as the end, and with the daily life of the true Mason as the means, have gained even the slightest insight into the true mysteries of the ancient rites.

With all the preceding in mind, and in the spirit of the fourth degree, I urge all of you who read this to treat this day in your Scottish Rite journey as a new beginning—an invitation to grow, and to travel beyond toleration.

Presentation to the Squirrel Hill Historical Society

The following are the written notes prepared for a presentation to the Squirrel Hill Historical Society, delivered July 10, 2018.

INTRODUCTION

I grew up in New York City in a conservative Jewish family (although not extremely observant). As a child I spent a good amount of time with my mother's parents and had a great affinity for my grandfather. He was silly and fun, but also a very intellectual man. He devoted himself to the practice of chiropractic care in an era when it really wasn't established yet. He also had an interest in Eastern medicine, philosophy, and other esoteric subjects. At some point, as a younger man, he had become involved with the Freemasons.

When I was in high school, I became interested in some of the esoteric subjects I first discovered in his library, and there eventually came a point where I asked him about the Freemasons. He said to me, "Well, you're about to go off to college; Freemasonry is a fraternity. Why don't you go see what the fraternal experience is like for yourself, and if it interests you we can discuss it more." But I know now that when he said that, he couldn't have had any idea how much Greek fraternities on college campuses had changed in the sixty years since he had been in college. So, I came to Pittsburgh to attend Carnegie Mellon University in 1993; and although I had fun delving into the college fraternity experience, I didn't see something of compelling value in it, so I didn't pursue membership in one of those, and I didn't discuss Freemasonry any further with my grandfather.

I didn't give it a lot of thought in the interim but when I did, I suspected that there must have been some disconnect in making that comparison. Thirteen years later, I had long since finished undergraduate and graduate school and was living and working in the South Side. I had put down roots in Pittsburgh—I had many friends in the neighborhood, including some of the business owners along the main drag of Carson Street. So, it piqued my curiosity when I was walking past the Carson Street Deli one day and saw a flier that was advertising a social gathering—"Come watch the pro bowl, eat hoagies, and shoot some pool"—and it was sponsored by several Masonic bodies.

I walked in and asked the owner, Eric, about this flyer in the window. He told me he had been a member for five years at that time, enjoyed it very much, and was fairly active in it. I shared with him the history of my inquiry to my grandfather, my experiences that followed, and my suspicion that the comparison he drew might not have supplied me the best analogy, and that I wanted to know more. Eric said, "Well why don't you come out to this event, see what you think of it and about the guys and if it interests you, we can certainly talk more."

I went to this event not really knowing what to expect—would they be like the Stonecutters from the Simpsons episode? But they turned out to be ordinary men, from a wide variety of backgrounds, who were really pleasant and easy to talk to. I had a great time. Sometime shortly thereafter, I told Eric this was something I would be happy to be a part of and asked him what sort of requirements there were. Asking him was, itself, the first step. This was how I first became involved in June 2006.

In the twelve years since then, I became a member of a Masonic lodge . . . then an officer in that lodge . . . then I led that lodge . . . and I have since traveled to visit many others, as well as joining other branches which we refer to as "appendant bodies." Tonight I will share with you my experience in these travels, and also use that as the basis to share with you the history of the organization.

REGULAR, OR "BLUE LODGE", FREEMASONRY

The factual history of Freemasonry is often commingled with lore and anecdote. I have based anything I deliver to you today on sources I consider reputable and will be happy to furnish those sources.

The most sound and plausible origin story I have encountered is this: we know there existed a guild of stone masons in England. Such a guild was an organization where a prospect might be apprenticed to learn a trade and become a skilled craftsman. Rather than resorting to legend, we can point to a specific manuscript to give us an understanding of how early such entities were organized. The oldest Masonic document in existence is a manuscript published in 1840 by Mr. James Orchard Halliwell, and thus often referred to as the Halliwell manuscript. It is also known as the Regius poem and is, in fact, in verse. Scholars date its authorship between 1390 and 1445.

What seems likely is that the guild, which was a fairly public entity, had within it a quasi-religious body, a fraternity; and that while the practical guild (what my cohort refer to as "operatives") lost their raison d'etre over time, that fraternity was kept alive underground, to survive the Reformation and reemerge to intrigue the "natural philosophers" of the Renaissance, or what we would call symbolic, or speculative, Masonry. It is by this route you find men like Elias Ashmole being initiated in 1646, men who have no interest in building actual stone edifices, but who want to learn the philosophy and symbolism that has been preserved and handed down.

In 1717, four lodges in London met with a few goals in mind: to create a joint, central body from among their members; draft a constitution for this new entity and organize some regular gatherings of it; and to declare some authority over the lodges of London (which at that time was some 3 square miles in area). This is how the lodges that once met at the Goose and Gridiron Alehouse, the Crown Alehouse, the Apple Tree Tavern, and the Rummer and Grapes Tavern formed the Premier Grand Lodge of England, the first such central authority in the world.

All Masonry in the US derives its pedigree from this United Grand Lodge of England. This is a quality we refer to as "regular," and a lodge that cannot trace its lineage back to this is "irregular." Pennsylvania, New York, and New Jersey were the first fraternities recognized in the US. We have a Grand Lodge for each state—there is no national governing body, although in the contemporary era the heads of these Grand Lodges will sometimes convene to share ideas and compare practices.

The Grand Lodge of Pennsylvania was founded in 1731, formed from what was once St. John's Lodge, which met in Tun Tavern (also considered the birthplace of the Marine Corps). It has been held at a few different physical locations since. The Free Quaker Meeting House at the corner of 5th and Arch Streets and the Pennsylvania State House (now known as Independence Hall) are the past locations that still stand.

Benjamin Franklin became a Mason in 1731 when he reached the minimum age at that time of twenty-five years old. His ascent through the ranks was astounding and he became Grand Master of Pennsylvania in 1734. While many are aware of his diplomatic work on behalf of the United States with the French, less commonly known are Franklin's Masonic ties in that country. He was in Paris in 1778 to help initiate the writer, historian, and philosopher, Voltaire, into Lodge Neuf Soeurs, a prominent lodge there that was significant in organizing aid for the American Revolution.

Today, we have a beautiful Grand Lodge building at One North Broad Street a national historic landmark. The architect was James Hamilton Windrim, and it was designed in the Norman Romanesque style. It was begun in 1868, when over 10,000 people assembled for the laying of the cornerstone. It was completed and dedicated in 1873. It contains themed lodge rooms emulating the cultures of Egypt, Greece, Italy, Germany, Spain, and France, as well as a library and museum, and is open to public tours. Currently, Pennsylvania Freemasons number over 95,000 members with over 400 lodges in 66 counties.

More specific to our region of the state, Lodge 45 is the oldest permanent lodge west of the Allegheny Mountains. This makes some sense on the surface, as the lodges are usually numbered in the order that they are "warranted" (that is to say, granted permission to form by a Grand Lodge). The wording for their claim is specific and careful because there is a long tradition of military lodges—warranted within the military unit that composes them and permitted to meet wherever they may be stationed—and such military lodges precede 45. Regimental Lodge #19 was warranted by the provincial Grand Lodge of Pennsylvania in May 1779 and held meetings at Fort Dunmore, later to become known as Fort Pitt. The last known Worshipful Master (President) of Regimental Lodge #19 became a charter member of Lodge 45.

There is anecdotal evidence that at one point in the 1790s, Lodge 45 was meeting in the Cross-Keys Tavern on Wood Street near the corner of "diamond alley" (now Forbes Avenue). In 1809, while some members of Lodge 45 were splintering off to form another, the ones remaining behind formulated a plan to erect their own building. They were deeded a perpetual lease by William McCullough and his wife, Jenett, to a space at the northwest corner of Wood Street and Fifth Avenue. A set of trustees executed the paperwork, attesting that they would hold the property for the benefit of the lodge.

Two years later, the lodge had successfully built a building on the spot in time to hold a special procession into their new building on St. John the Baptist's day (June 24) in 1811, to which they invited the members of Lodge 113 to join them. Lodge 113 met very nearby, on the southeast corner of the "Diamond" (what we now refer to as Market Square). In August 1815, the members of Lodge 113 began to explore the notion of sharing space with Lodge 45 instead. They ended up sharing the new space until 1818, when they became interested in again having a space of their own. After a false start elsewhere, they ended up in the upper floor of the warehouse belonging to one William B. Foster, one of the members. By the fall of 1822, Lodge 45 was looking to move in with Lodge 113 instead and discussed how to dispose of their building on Fifth and Wood. They decided to sell it to Mr. Benjamin Darlington (father of member and past Master of McCandless Lodge 390, also Benjamin Darlington).

Mr. Darlington proceeds to use the building as an addition to Darlington's Hotel, also at the corner of Fifth and Wood. Herein lies another lovely bit of history—when Masonic brother and beloved war hero General Lafayette came through Pittsburgh on his victory tour in 1825, he stayed in the room that was originally occupied by the lodge. According to a quote from one of Darlington's sons, "The room in which Lafayette slept at the Mansion House, to my boyish notions, was one of the most magnificent ever constructed.

It had for many years been the Lodge Room of the Free Masons. The ceiling was arched, painted with figures of the sun, moon and stars. When the Masonic lease expired, the decorations were allowed to remain." The misconception about lease versus sale notwithstanding, it is heartwarming to me to think of Lafayette spending the night in these arrangements. Today, there is a brass plaque on the very spot, which is now One PNC Tower downtown, that reads, "This building marks the site of the hotel where Lafayette lodged from May 30 to June 1, 1825 on his tour as the nation's guest. The tavern was known as the mansion house and was removed about 1838."

Meanwhile, Lodge 45 apparently shared space with 113 and 165 for some time along with two York Rite bodies. But in 1823 all the lodges began collaboration on the idea of building their own entire building. At the time it came to no fruition, nor did similar rumblings in 1826. In 1829, however, an opportunity arose when two furniture manufacturers, Mr. McGill of Lodge 45 and Mr. Darsie of Lodge 165, proposed to build a building for their business on the corner of Smithfield Street and Third Avenue, and to allow the Freemasons the use of the upstairs. They assumed occupancy of that space sometime in the summer of 1830 and were there until the Great Fire of Pittsburgh on April 10, 1845, in which the building and most contents were destroyed.

A mere five days later, they met at the office of Brother Samuel McKinley to discuss what to do and were visited by a contingent from another fraternal organization, the International Order of Odd Fellows, who kindly invited them to make use of their space at the southeast corner of Wood

Street and Virgin Alley (now known as Oliver Avenue). The Masons sent a small group to assess the suitability of such a proposal, and the invitation was accepted. But this was only ever viewed as a temporary fix, and with two new lodges constituted in 1846, St. Johns #219 and Franklin #221, the Masons soon had their eye on building their own location yet again. In 1850 they built a temple on Fifth Street downtown (later to be named Fifth Avenue) on land purchased from a member and real estate dealer, George R. Riddle.

The first floor housed some businesses, the second, a venue for lectures and concerts, and the third was reserved for Masonic activities. In April 1851, P.T. Barnum brought the vocalist Jenny Lind, the "Swedish Nightingale," to Pittsburgh with all the fanfare of today's pop stars. Further renovations to the building were needed just to accommodate her performance. Some 7,000 or 8,000 people never even made it into the hall.

The beloved venue remained the meeting place for several of Pittsburgh's Masonic bodies until the night of August 12, 1887, when this location, too, was destroyed by fire. Very little was able to be recovered—a few of the officers' insignias that hang from ribbon collars, which at the present day are in a display case at the Greater Pittsburgh Masonic Center; a Seth Thomas clock; and a partly wrecked officer's chair, from whose oak remains, three canes were made and distributed to members. Thanks to the unusual cautiousness of their lodge master, Harry D.W. English, their warrant had been kept in his office safe and was also preserved. The lodge continues to keep the warrant in a customized container that appears at their meetings.

The day immediately following the fire, one of the local Scottish Rite Masonic bodies (which I will explain at more length shortly) stepped in to convene a meeting of the current officers of the lodges who had lost their building, to coordinate efforts to relocate (and many past officers attended as well). They cooperated to rent space in the Renshaw Building at the corner of Liberty Avenue and Ninth Street, which was sufficient to their purposes as a temporary arrangement. However, they were determined to rebuild at the very same location on Fifth Street. As Freemasonry draws its history and symbolism from architecture and construction, it has particular ceremonies that ought to accompany the laying of cornerstones. On September 11, 1888, a new cornerstone was laid, in a solemn ceremony including officers from our Grand Lodge in Philadelphia, that began with a procession to the site consisting of 1,450 Masons. By April 1889, Masons were meeting at the downtown Fifth Street site again.

They remained at that site until 1915, when a new building was built in Oakland. That temple was constructed from 1914 to 1915, and the architect was Benno Janssen (also responsible for the William Penn Hotel and the Mellon Institute). In 1993, the University of Pittsburgh proposed a generous offer to the trustees of the building, which they considered in the best interests of the organization to accept. The Masons were permitted to continue their use of the facilities while construction of the new location took place, on Cemetery Lane in Ross Township, which would be referred to as the Greater Pittsburgh Masonic Center. The cornerstone ritual there was conducted by the Grand Lodge of Pennsylvania on October 9, 1995, and the construction concluded in the fall of 1996. The former temple was designated a landmark by the Pittsburgh History and Landmarks Foundation in 2002 and is now University of Pittsburgh's alumni hall.

Now, I imagine I could come off as a biased presenter of this subject matter, as a member of these organizations who would be disposed to present them in a positive light. But I do believe the study of history ought to remain as objective as possible; and it is in this spirit that I will share with you some information about a darker episode in the history of Freemasonry in the US and its specific significance for Pennsylvania and Pittsburgh.

It began, in part, with a man by the name of William Morgan, born in Culpeper County, Virginia, in 1774. In his travels in upstate New York in the 1820s, he visited several blue lodges claiming to be a member and was believed. In 1825, he had one of the York Rite (appendant body) degrees conferred upon him in LeRoy, NY, shortly following which, he signed a petition calling for the creation of a new chapter in the town of Batavia, NY, where he was residing. However, some members in Batavia who were uncertain of his character (and some, of the veracity of his claims of membership) chose to exclude him by crossing out his name on the petition. Stung by the insult (although his debts may also have contributed to commercial motivations), Morgan struck a deal with a receptive printer, David C. Miller, to publish an expose of Masonic secrets—something antithetical to Masonic principles.

When word got out around Buffalo, Canandaigua, LeRoy, Lewiston, Lockport, and Rochester, the area Masons were scandalized. They knew divulging the secrets of the organization is strictly prohibited, and they might have been further upset were they aware that such materials had already been published abroad and could be had in the US. In defense of the fraternity, they planned to thwart the publication. Their efforts began with harassment and threats, which proved ineffective. On September 10, 1826, someone tried and failed to burn down Miller's print shop. In the days that followed, a warrant was issued for Morgan's arrest on charges of stealing a shirt and cravat from an innkeeper in May of that year. He was taken into custody, brought to Canandaigua, released for lack of evidence, and promptly rearrested for a rather small debt to another innkeeper. But this he admitted to, so he went back into incarceration. That night, in the absence of the jailer, three Masons convinced the jailer's wife to release Morgan upon payment of the debt. She subsequently witnessed Morgan being abducted by four unidentified men, and he was never heard from again. This incident, along with accusations of cronyism among Masons in government or other positions of authority, catalyzed a movement that led to the first viable third party in American politics, the Anti-Masonic party.

One very active figure in the Anti-Masonic party was Thaddeus Stevens. As a teacher at an academy in York, PA, who went on to practice law, he had a deep-seated mistrust of secret societies and placed a premium on egalitarianism and objectivity in the justice system. His career in the party kicked off in 1829 when he worked to coordinate efforts in Adams County, founded the *Gettysburg Star*, and was a booster for Joseph Ritner for governor.

Ritner, from Berks County in eastern Pennsylvania, was the child of poor German immigrants. He had enough success as a wool weaver to secure horses and a wagon and move himself west, to Washington County. He was elected to the House of Representatives in 1820 and was honored with the role of speaker in 1824 and 1825. Although it's uncertain what aligned him with the movement, it is possible it related to opposition to Jackson on an 1827 tariff bill that raised rates on wool. In his several campaigns for governor against George Wolf, a Jacksonian Democrat and prominent Mason, Ritner was defeated in 1829 and 1832, eventually succeeding in 1835.

One other success of the Anti-Masonic party was personified by Harmar Denny, the son of Pittsburgh's mayor, who carried Allegheny, Armstrong, Beaver, and Butler counties to be elected to the US House of Representatives in 1824. As an Anti-Masonic candidate, he served three terms in Congress from 1829 to 1837. While the power of the Anti-Masonic party began to decline after 1832, it was still considered a significant force in terms of its endorsement of a candidate, especially for the Whig nominees. Accordingly, in the 1836 presidential contest between Daniel Webster and William Henry Harrison, Webster was heavily courting the party. Having persuaded Webster to come out with a staunchly anti-Masonic statement, Denny gave him a pretty clear indication it would likely result in endorsement. However, in spite of Denny being selected as presiding officer at their state nominating convention, the delegates splintered into factions, and the vote went to Harrison instead. By their next national convention in 1838, the party was perceived as having been, more or less, subsumed by the Whigs.

While the presence of the Anti-Masonic party on the American political scene was relatively short-lived, I acknowledge as valid the concerns of a general public "on the outside looking in" and what the perceptions of Masonic allegiance could be. And because I was aware of the Morgan affair before I joined, I wondered whether that episode had relevant implications for what I was contemplating getting involved in. But I was convinced my grandfather would never have enlisted in something unsavory, and I didn't have the impression that Eric would either.

From the beginning of my experience, I looked to Eric for guidance in how to proceed. A person could certainly focus time and energy to delve deeper into the experience of the main organization of Masonry, colloquially referred to as "blue lodge," a nickname for which I have heard interesting anecdotal explanations, but I'm not convinced I've heard one definitive one. Eric, however, had chosen to diversify his pursuits among several of the appendant bodies—organizations for which membership in blue lodge is a prerequisite—and so I followed suit. He seemed especially pleased that my initiation in blue lodge concluded one month before a window to join the Scottish Rite, another group in which he was active. So, in November 2006, I joined.

THE SCOTTISH RITE

A first important fact to recognize is that Scottish Rite Masonry is not Scottish in origin; it is French. In the eighteenth century, the French performed a few Masonic degrees beyond the three common to the standard system (this baseline usually being referred to as "craft lodge" or "blue lodge" Masonry). Although these higher degrees varied a bit in their content from place to place, there was one fairly universal one, which bore the title of Ecossais (French for "Scottish"), which later became the moniker for the entire set of higher degrees.

In 1761, a fellow by the name of Etienne Morin was granted a document giving him a mandate to regulate any craft lodges under this French Grand Lodge throughout the world, including their holdings in the Western Hemisphere. As a trader who traveled, he was well-suited for this role. It is believed that at some time while having this document duplicated, he also embellished upon it, attributing to himself authority over the higher degrees as well. He also composed documents to organize and govern these bodies, and in 1762 returned to San Domingo (since renamed the Dominican Republic).

There, he deputized Henry Francken. Francken helped Morin document the rituals and was steeped in the degrees; and subsequently it was he who brought the content to America (not yet even its own nation). This was the source of the Ineffable Lodge of Perfection, opened in Albany, NY, in October 1767 and offered degrees 4 through 25. But by late 1774 the Albany body had lost its momentum and closed shop. There were a few other abortive starts like this—in Philadelphia from 1782 to 1789 and in Charleston, SC, from 1783 to 1796.

On May 31, 1801, a group of members convened in Charleston dubbing themselves "The Supreme Council 33° of Freemasonry," led by Colonel John Mitchell and Reverend Dr.

Frederick Dalcho, two veterans of the Revolutionary War. Among the others in attendance were Isaac Auld, a prominent physician and Dalcho's associate; Comte De-Grasse Tilly, the son of a French admiral; Jean-Baptiste Marie de La Hogue, the Comte's father-in-law; Thomas Bartholomew Bowen, a printer; Abraham Alexander, Emmanuel De La Motta, and Isaac Da Costa, all Sephardic Jews; Israel De Lieben, also Jewish, who emigrated to the US from Prague at the age of twenty-one; Moses Clava Levy, a prosperous Polish merchant; and James Moultrie, also a physician.

While this marked the beginning of a healthy settled and organized phase for Scottish Rite Masonry in the southern US, matters were in evident disarray in the north. Three competing groups were claiming ultimate authority in New York—one headed up by a Joseph Cerneau, who had received the degrees in Cuba, another led by Antoine Bideaud, who had become active in the higher degrees in the French West Indies, and yet another led by Abraham Jacobs, who had gotten his charter in Jamaica. The Southern body sent De La Motta to investigate the situation and determine the legitimacy or validity of each of these and recommend what ought to be done.

Having approached all three in 1813, De La Motta's findings can be summarized as follows: Cerneau's group was entirely uncooperative with the investigation; Jacobs' organization lacked the appropriate establishing documents; and Bideaud's group was found compliant and deemed the equal of the Charleston group for what would later become known as the Northern Masonic Jurisdiction of the United States of America. Daniel D. Tompkins, who had served as secretary of the group and was Governor of New York at the time, became the first Sovereign Grand Commander, and John James Joseph Gourgas was the first Grand Secretary.

In 1911, the Southern Jurisdiction broke ground on a new headquarters, the House of the Temple in Washington, DC. The architect on the project was John Russell Pope, and he emulated the tomb of Mausolus at Helicarnassus, one of the seven wonders of the world, which Henry Hornbostel had also taken as his inspiration for the Soldiers & Sailors memorial in Pittsburgh in 1908. The construction was completed in 1915 and it contained the first public library in Washington, DC. It also contains the remains of Masonic author and luminary Albert Pike, who was reinterred there in 1944 when his remains were moved from Oak Hill Cemetery in the Georgetown neighborhood.

The Northern Jurisdiction began in 1813 by holding meetings in various locations around New York. Their operations were significantly disrupted by a scandal in 1826 that led to the formation of the first third party in American politics, the Anti-Masonic party. The negative public sentiment persisted until around 1844, and the activities of the Northern Supreme Council were maintained largely by the heroic efforts of J.J.J. Gourgas, the secretary mentioned earlier (in honor of which, one of the Pittsburgh bodies is named after him—the very group that would step in to shepherd the Pittsburgh lodges in the wake of the fire in 1887). Throughout the 1840s, they convened in various quarters provided by the Grand Lodge of New York, but in summer of 1845 they appear to have met in Boston. Meeting minutes from 1851 indicate that the headquarters were now officially moved to the Grand Lodge building in Boston, even though the secretary remained in New York. In 1927, the body relocated to the Statler Building in Park Square in Boston, and having outgrown that by the 1960s, relocated to a beautiful property in Lexington, MA, where it resides to this day.

While each blue lodge typically serves the city or town in which it is located, the Scottish Rite is organized in such a fashion that there is one body that draws its membership from many surrounding lodges within a larger radius. The body is dubbed a "valley." The Valley of Pittsburgh was established in the 1840s and was used to meet in the Temple on Fifth Avenue between Tennyson and Lytton in the Oakland neighborhood (which we also discussed was the home of Lodge 45). Today, they are both located in the Greater Pittsburgh Masonic Center, off Cemetery Lane in Ross.

Now, as I have said, my friend Eric pursued many of the different side routes available to a member who has completed his standard three degrees in the blue lodge; and I was curious enough about exploring these options that I wanted to follow in his footsteps, to the extent I was able. However, my curiosity about what one could learn via these experiences, combined with a feeling of duty to serve and support the groups I felt I derived so much from, led me to pursue leadership positions, in both the blue lodge and the Scottish Rite. I was certainly grateful that others showed some confidence in my ability to contribute something of value in such roles. While I was eager to continue my exploration of the other appendant bodies, I believed I wouldn't have adequate time and attention to do so until my obligations in these first two were completed. I led my blue lodge,

Tyrian #644, as its Worshipful Master, finishing my term in December 2013; and I led one of the four groups that collaborate to govern the Valley of Pittsburgh, known as the Princes of Jerusalem, as its Sovereign Prince, finishing my term in the summer of 2015.

The appendant bodies once adhered to an arrangement, where a member could pursue membership in the Shrine only after he had completed the whole course of either Scottish Rite or York Rite. Although this requirement was abandoned in 2000, I was attracted to the idea of joining the group in the sequence it had been done historically and joined in November 2014.

SHRINERS INTERNATIONAL

The Shrine as an organization was created by Masons in New York City in 1870. Walter M. Fleming and William J. Florence were members of a luncheon club called the Knickerbocker Cottage at 456 6th Avenue. Florence, a famous actor, had participated in a party game at a gathering hosted by an Arabian diplomat, the finale of which purported to initiate the guests into a (satirical) secret society. Florence and Fleming had already discussed the notion of an organizational offshoot, less focused on philosophy, ethics, and symbolism, and more so on recreation and mirth. Fleming took Florence's notes regarding his experience and crafted the ritual, seal, and middle-eastern garb they would use.

They also enlisted Charles T. McClenachan, a renowned lawyer and Masonic ritualist, and William Paterson, a prosperous local printer. These two, along with nine other men, were initiated on June 16, 1871. We also know they met at New York's Masonic Hall at 114 East 13th Street on September 26, 1872, for the purpose of formally organizing themselves and electing officers. However, the new organization did not take off in leaps and bounds; four years later, there were still only forty-three members, and all but six of them were from New York City.

Oddly enough, the catalyst that took the Shrine into high gear seems to have been the creation of a national governing body, backwards though that might sound. In June 1876, thirty of the members met again at New York's Masonic Hall, this time initiating twenty-five new members. At a subsequent meeting to conduct the business of the organization, Fleming motioned for the creation of a national governing body to be called the Imperial Grand Council.

Fleming, who had valiantly shouldered much of the burden up to this point, was elected the first Grand Potentate ("Potentate" being the honorific for the president of an individual Shrine location, and "Grand" being the prefix we usually attach for someone leading a national body). Notably, Samuel Harper, who would at one point be Potentate of Pittsburgh's Syria Shrine, was elected the first Grand Marshall. This was also the meeting at which the resolution requiring Shriners to also be members in good standing of either the York Rite or Scottish Rite was enacted.

In 1877, three men from Pittsburgh received their Shrine initiation at Mecca Temple in NYC: Alexander Rook, William Ramsey, and Samuel Wainright. Upon their return, they met with other members in the living room of George Balmain to discuss pursuing a charter for their own Shrine Temple. On May 19, 1877, their labors came to fruition and the charter was granted. Ten days later, they were electing the officers who would govern Syria Temple, including Samuel Harper as our potentate, who served in that capacity until 1884.

Meanwhile, on the national stage, in 1888, twelve new temples were chartered, and the Imperial Council (which had dropped "Grand" from its name two years hence) convened in Toronto—the first meeting outside of the US. Members from Pittsburgh continued to appear in the national governing body—Past Potentate Thomas Hudson became Imperial Potentate in 1893 and Past Potentate William Brown labored in the role of Imperial Treasurer. By 1899 there were seventy-eight temples. In 1906, membership surpassed 100,000 men and by 1922, it would exceed 511,000.

For some time, Syria temple conducted its functions in Library Hall. Subsequently, they had a base of operations for some time in Turner Hall on Forbes Street until 1902. They then built their first building of their own on Washington Street, where they operated until 1911, when they sold that building and used the proceeds to buy property in Schenley Farms. Although there was a sluggish phase in the life of Syria Shrine from 1910 to 1912, when a committee contacted the membership in 1913 with plans for a new building, it spurred the members into action and they pledged sufficient funds to begin the construction. Two Shriners, Harris Huehl and Charles Rieger, were brought on as the architects.

The groundbreaking took place on April 20, 1915, at a location we now consider 4223 Bigelow Boulevard. Construction was finished the following year and the building dedicated with a weeklong extravaganza that began October 23, 1916. Monday was devoted to the Shriners; Tuesday, to all Masons; Wednesday, to the general public; Thursday was set aside for a dedication ceremony; on Friday, a ball was held for members and their ladies; and Saturday was reserved for the children. Some 40,000 people are reported to have attended.

The auditorium at the mosque seated approximately 3,500 people and, as became common at many Shrine facilities elsewhere, was rented as a performance venue by musical acts when not in use by the membership. Many Pittsburghers can regale you with nostalgic reminiscences of fondly remembered concerts they attended at this venue. What they might not know, is that the Syria mosque was also considered the birthplace of network television, as it was there that DuMont Television Network (later to become KDKA-TV) made its first broadcast over a network of cables connecting thirteen cities on the evening of January 11, 1949.

No history of the Shrine would be complete without mention of the Shriners' hospitals for children. When the Imperial body convened in Portland, OR, in 1920, a resolution was passed to create what was then dubbed the Shriners Hospital for Crippled Children system. The first hospital providing pediatric orthopedic care was opened in Shreveport, LA, in 1922. In 1962, the Shriners of North America earmarked $10 million to found three hospitals dedicated to treating pediatric burn victims.

Meanwhile, in Pittsburgh, the Shriners were faced with a familiar problem in the 1980s—a building in decline. The mosque in Oakland was put up for sale in June 1989 and was razed in August 1991. In October 1994, the new Shrine Center in Cheswick was born—a $10 million, 40,000-square-foot facility. Set on 37 acres, the building is accompanied by a proportionate amount of parking, a tremendous covered pavilion, and a wonderful playground for children. The driveway to the building is flanked by twin sphinxes that made the journey from the original building, as did the enormous chandeliers in the ballroom.

By this point in my own history, I had truly developed an appetite and curiosity to explore the various branches of Freemasonry through the appendant bodies. Eric told me that many interesting avenues also began via the York Rite. The York Rite had earlier appeared as some kind of contrast or alternative to the Scottish Rite that one had to choose between; however, as I continued to travel, it became clear that a fair number of people belonged to both. I had heard some intriguing snippets about individual degrees or aspects (which one may also uncover with determined Googling, but I really ought not to reveal). I came to the conclusion that I was interested in pursuing this route also. So, on Saturday, October 3, 2015, I received my first two degrees in a Royal Arch Chapter at the Penn Hills Masonic Center; and on the 17th of the same month, I made a road trip with the members to the Washington Masonic Memorial in Alexandria, VA, to receive the Royal Arch degree in a lodge room there.

THE YORK RITE

York Rite Masonry as it currently exists in the US is essentially a result of a schism in the Grand Lodge of England.

I hope you will recall my earlier description of the origins of the Premier Grand Lodge of England, a collaboration of four lodges in London, in 1717. To keep a long story short, in 1751, a splinter group called into question the effectiveness of the body in faithfully maintaining the traditions. Accordingly, they spun off, calling themselves the "Antients" (as in preserving ancient ways) and referred derogatively to the group they left behind as the "Moderns" (as in introducing modern innovations). Sadly, an acrimonious division persisted until reconciliation was finally achieved in 1813, which is why the resulting body, which has subsisted to this day, renamed itself the United Grand Lodge of England. The term "York Rite," until this point, had referred to the manner in which ordinary blue lodge initiation was conducted. However, in the process of settling upon what would be included from that day forward, some well-loved material was now delegated to new and separate bodies. In the US, those bodies and degrees would come to be referred to as the York Rite, although considered to be transformed from its European origins and a product of American enthusiasm for "higher degrees."

In our system, the York Rite consists of three bodies: Chapter of Royal Arch Masons, Council of Cryptic Masons, and Commandery of Knights Templar (commonly abbreviated as Chapter, Council, and Commandery). There are chapters and councils in quite a few cities and towns, operating with similar logistics to an individual lodge. Commanderies are slightly more dispersed, depending on the other two bodies for membership, as they are prerequisites.

York Rite has deep roots in Pennsylvania. Regarding Chapter, the Grand Lodge of England (Antients) issued a warrant for Lodge #3 in Philadelphia in 1758. Their minutes in 1767 make reference to possessing the necessary costumes and props for conferring the Royal Arch degree, and refer to it as such. When they finally adopted bylaws in 1789, they also named officers appropriate to conducting that work. There was some disruption in 1795 when a fraudulent member, James Molan, turned up on the scene and proceeded to create new chapters—even a Grand Chapter for the state! At this point, the Grand Lodge of Pennsylvania stepped in, suspended the impostor's activities, and created a proper Grand Chapter for Pennsylvania under the authority of the Grand Lodge of the same.

Regarding Council, a Grand Council for Pennsylvania was created by two councils here and with the aid of one from Texas in 1847. Some of their meeting minutes from subsequent years have been uncovered. In 1854, a peculiar suggestion was floated to surrender the authority for the Cryptic degrees to one of the Scottish Rite bodies (the Princes of Jerusalem). This did not succeed and the Grand body was reorganized in December of that year. Both Chapter and Council for Pennsylvania have maintained independence from General Grand bodies, meta-groups where the grand bodies of multiple states confer together, of their respective organizations.

Regarding Commandery, Pennsylvania can lay claim to having created the first Grand Encampment of Knights Templar on May 12, 1797 (also unsurprisingly in Philadelphia). At the time it had four subordinates that answered to its authority—#1 and #2 in Philadelphia, #3 in Harrisburg, and #4 in Carlisle. The two Philadelphia Commanderies merged under #1 in 1812 and, with the collaboration of a new #2 in Pittsburgh, created a new Grand Encampment in February 1814. This lasted ten years, at which time owing to anti-Masonic sentiment in the country (which I will still elaborate upon), the Templars in Pennsylvania had been winnowed down to St. John's encampment #4 in Philadelphia, which was simply operating under the Grand Lodge (the governing body for blue lodge). As the Rite revived in 1852, St. John's was able to band together with Philadelphia #5, Union #6, and DeMolay (a youth group) based in Reading. However, the Grand Lodge deemed it inappropriate that they should wield authority over the Templar degrees, and in 1857, a new Grand Encampment was formed. Unlike Chapter and Council, the Grand Encampment of Pennsylvania is affiliated with a national body.

I can go into quite a bit of detail regarding the history of my specific Royal Arch Chapter, as they saw fit on their 100th anniversary (in 1988) to publish a book on the subject. And because it was, in reality, created by the merger of three different chapters, this history actually offers a broader survey than one might initially suspect, covering three different Pittsburgh neighborhoods, and touches on interesting shared topics and events with other branches along the way.

It all began in January 1888 when the secretaries of two lodges, William J. Diehl of Hailman Lodge #321 and Archie K. Henderson of Duquesne Lodge #546, circulated a letter to the attention of current Royal Arch Masons inviting them to a planning meeting for a new chapter to meet in East

Liberty. It is fair to infer this was a more prominent and bustling time for Freemasonry in general, when there was enough membership that people were creating new units. A meeting was held on February 6 and officers were chosen to head up the new Chapter. From several alternatives, it was decided to simply name the Chapter "Pittsburgh." The necessary permission from the Grand body was secured, and the officers of Grand Chapter arrived themselves on April 30 to perform the fitting ceremonies to create Pittsburgh Royal Arch Chapter #268.

In Homewood, during the second half of 1912, eight brothers gathered signatures from forty-six fellow Royal Arch members for a petition to submit to Grand Chapter of Pennsylvania to create a chapter in Homewood. Zerubbabel Chapter #162 and Pittsburgh Chapter #268 donated $200 apiece, a hefty sum in that era, to support the cause. So it was that on October 28, 1913, Homewood Royal Arch Chapter #297 was constituted at the Homewood Masonic Hall, at 7226 Kelly Street. Thirty-eight charter members, twenty-two visitors, and various officials and dignitaries were in attendance. Homewood initiated sixty candidates by the end of 1914. Two years later, their membership was 167. Two years later still, they numbered 213. By the end of 1920, they had 290 members. That's a compound annual growth rate of 34% a year.

Meanwhile, in Braddock, several members of Braddock's Field Lodge #510 were desirous of creating their own Royal Arch Chapter as well. Although their lodge building was not yet suitably outfitted for the ritual work, they were able to make the necessary renovations. They also felt they had the appropriate personnel at hand, having some existing

Chapter members as well as blue lodge officers who at least had experience with memorizing dialogue. Seven main instigators of the action met to discuss planning and five agreed to take on some of the main roles in administrating the new body. Accordingly, on June 26, 1917, members of the Grand Chapter traveled to 428–430 Library Street in Braddock, PA, for the purpose of constituting Braddock's Field Royal Arch Chapter #303.

Several notes I found in the history of each chapter undoubtedly applied to all three, in the way that these groups are governed and conduct themselves. In 1889, Pittsburgh Chapter got a letter, jointly signed by Grand Lodge and Grand Chapter, to shun the illegitimate Masonic bodies under Cerneau. They also made a donation to the chapter in Johnstown for flood relief; made an order in 1915 that singing "The Star-Spangled Banner" would become part of the standard opening of meetings; and, the time in October 1918, when bodies complied with an order from the state board of health not to meet, in order to impede the spread of Spanish Flu.

There are some notes in the histories of these chapters that are quite unique and distinctive. I took particular note of the fact that in 1938, when there was clearly a lull in the quantity of new members inducted, Homewood Chapter #297 brought in only five members. Four of these were initiated in a specially organized "class" and given their three Royal Arch degrees in one day on March 10. One noteworthy aspect was that one of Homewood's own past presiding officers who had ascended to an office in the Grand line, and James C. Weir was there to confer one of the degrees. Another noteworthy aspect was that one of the candidates that day was Cornelius Scully, mayor of the city of Pittsburgh.

The context of that event points to one factor that all three chapters were certainly subject to the ebb and flow of membership. All three experienced significant growth after World War I; they were impacted by members' inability to keep up with dues during the Great Depression; and there was also an impact on the organization with many men leaving to fight during World War II. Over time, all three chapters were confronting the challenge of how to keep themselves vital. In August 1946, the trustees of Pittsburgh Royal Arch Chapter met to plan selling and leaving their property in East Liberty and moving into the temple on 5th Avenue in Oakland; and in April 1963, Homewood Chapter moved from their location at 7226 Kelly Street to the Wilkinsburg Masonic Temple at 747 South Avenue. They later concluded that these efforts only led to further decline in interest (which we get to read with the benefit of 20/20 hindsight), which, therefore, led to their later move to the East Hills Masonic Temple at 5793 Saltsburg Road, which was decided in May 1965 and executed in August 1965.

So it goes, that on September 9, 1974, a motion was introduced in a meeting of Pittsburgh Chapter #268 by member and past presiding officer Raymond Wert that they merge with the other two chapters under the new name East Hills, meeting at the East Hills Masonic Temple and retaining the oldest number of the three (#268). While the East Hills Royal Arch Chapter of today may not presently match the membership numbers of the heyday of the chapters that combined to form it at 172 members as of June 2018 we do our best to honor those forebears by presenting ritual faithfully and enjoying the warmth of our fellowship.

Given the trends we have discussed regarding membership levels in the branches of Freemasonry, as groups decline and merge or cease operations, you can imagine it's somewhat uncommon to see the creation of a brand new unit. So, when Eric approached me in late 2015 to discuss creating a chapter of Allied Masonic Degrees, I knew that what he was sharing represented an unusual opportunity, generally speaking. But what specifically was the purpose of the organization? (And was there enough to it, to justify joining something else?)

THE ALLIED MASONIC DEGREES

The Allied Masonic Degrees grew out of a study group of Masons in Monroe, NC, who met up throughout the late 1920s and early 1930s, often at the home of brother J. Raymond Shute II. In 1930, he initiated communications with the secretary of one of the York Rite grand bodies in Scotland, George A. Howell, regarding one of the degrees performed in Scotland but not yet in the US. Permission was granted by the Earl of Cassillis to confer the degree at the grand body in Asheville, NC, on May 12, 1931, where about 200 Royal Arch Masons received the degree of Excellent Master.

The warm response of the American Masons to this activity led to further conjecture about how to make the degree permanently available stateside, and import others from Scotland, without infringing on York Rite activities as already organized here. With a great deal of communication back and forth to solicit clearance from the proper Masonic authorities in North Carolina and Scotland, Howell consented to grant the request of three units in the US on the condition that they would foster their own grand body at their earliest convenience. Charters were granted at the annual meeting of the Supreme Grand Royal Arch Chapter of Scotland on March 21, 1932, for the creation of the first three chapters in the US: St Andrews in America #1A (Monroe, NC), Cassillis #2A (Raleigh, NC), and Howell #3A (Charlotte, NC). True to the arrangement, on April 16 of the same year, they convened in Salisbury, NC, to create the Grand Council of Allied Masonic Degrees of the USA. At the Salisbury meeting it was also agreed upon to hold another gathering in Washington, DC, in May, during a celebration of George Washington's bicentennial.

Five new councils were created by the time the Washington, DC, meeting took place. So, the Grand Council had their first official annual meeting a year later on May 8, 1933, in Charlotte, where there was much business to conduct: they chartered three more councils, organized a newsletter for the publishing of research papers, created an honorary rank to bestow on the twenty-one founding members, and adopted the constitution and bylaws proposed at the gathering in Washington, DC.

Not long after the meeting in Charlotte, however, it came to light that some of the degrees this Grand Council of AMD was offering had formerly been performed in the US by a group in Norway, ME, called the Sovereign Grand College of Allied and Christian Degrees. It was founded by an Episcopal rector and Masonic leader named Hartley Carmichael, along with Josiah Drummond and Charles Nesbitt, in Richmond, VA, in 1882. The materials and proceedings of the organization had moved to Maine when Carmichael and Nesbitt passed away and it was on its last legs; but its predating this Grand Council called their authority over those degrees somewhat into question. In July 1933, Shute and a companion, William Mosely Brown, traveled to Norway, ME, and drew up an agreement to fold the Allied and Christian Degrees into the Grand Council. This was formally adopted July 22, 1933, at a special session in Raleigh NC, giving them clear right to the duplicated degrees, and adding new ones to the roster as well.

So, it would be worth pointing out here that, in the time since I have joined the Masons, ritual has been a significant focus for me. In some groups, this amounts to memorized lectures, a somewhat solitary activity. In others, the ritual is presented in a theatrical fashion and involves rehearsals and more interaction with other performers. In either case it is something I enjoy, so when the focus of Allied Masonic Degrees (AMD) on even more obscure ritual was explained to me, I was rather intrigued; and the opportunity to be a founding member certainly heightened the appeal.

It was with those interests in mind that I showed up at a planning meeting at the Masonic Temple in Washington, PA, on January 9, 2016, to discuss with ten other men the details and logistics for forming our own Council of AMD (I have the meeting notes open in front of me as I write this presentation). We discussed existing councils in the Mon Valley, Turtle Creek, Butler, and Claysville, and how we intended to differentiate ourselves; how to get in touch with the governing authority to request necessary permission; our beginning slate of officers; and where and when we would meet (for which we settled upon the Masonic Hall in Uniontown).

There was an interval of delay as some of our communication required an in-person follow-up at an annual gathering out-of-state. However, on March 26, 2017, we assembled in Uniontown, accompanied by our guest Erastus Allen, the Grand Superintendent for Western Pennsylvania as the representative from Grand Council who delivered our document declaring us official, performed the accompanying ceremony, and installed our officers in their stations. Since then, we have held two other meetings (and one dinner); initiated two brand new members; accepted one member for plural membership (i.e., affiliating with our council while maintaining membership in another); and received positive feedback on our efforts from guests who visit us from other chapters. I serve this group as their secretary. It has been a pleasure banding together with people I have known for a decade, to embark on this journey of creating something new. Writing about it for this presentation makes it feel a bit like stepping into history.

The last body I joined was the Tall Cedars. By this time, my brother Eric had promised me he wasn't going to ask me to join anything else. Perhaps I should have suspected the campaign wasn't quite over. But at the time, he was simply inviting me to a dinner function that was open to guests who were not members—an evening to celebrate his completion of a year governing his unit. However, as I sat eating my spaghetti, I suddenly found myself hemmed in by Eric and another member, and he said to me, "Austin, I'm wondering if you can help us out—we're kind of in a bind." Always willing to help my buddy, I asked him what the trouble was. When he explained to me that the current state of their progression of officers left a vacancy at the bottom rung that nobody expressed an interest in occupying, I sighed with resignation and told him to pass me a petition. That is how on Wednesday, Oct 4, 2017, I was both initiated into the Tall Cedars of Lebanon and elected Junior Deputy Grand Tall Cedar.

THE TALL CEDARS OF LEBANON

Tall Cedars is an appendant body, organized in units called a "forest," much like an individual blue lodge. There are thirty-four forests in Pennsylvania, and each forest is run by three officers in a progressive line: a Grand Tall Cedar, and his Senior Deputy and Junior Deputy Grand Tall Cedars. We are in a district with Elizabeth, Uniontown, Washington, and Latrobe, and then a region, that further connects us with Kittanning, Meadville, Newcastle, and Pittsford, NY (a suburb of Rochester). Presently, there are approximately 10,000 members nationally.

The Tall Cedars of Lebanon has our origins dating to 1843, according to the late J. Edward Bullen, who was our Supreme Historian from 1970 to 1975. Unfortunately, the innovators' names seem to be lost to the mists of time; it got its start as a humorous degree, conferred immediately after the close of blue lodge, and consisted of some roughhousing and hazing (I can assure you it is more genteel now). At that time, the degree was entitled "The Ancient and Honorable

Rite of Humility." The most specific intelligence we have is regarding Dr. Thomas J. Corson, who received the degree in Philadelphia and returned to his native New Jersey to confer it throughout the early 1850s, around which time the briefer title of "Tall Cedar Degree" prevailed. In 1864, Bro. William H. Adams, Grand Secretary of the Grand Lodge of Pennsylvania, captured the ritual and some observations in writing and it remains in the archives of our Grand Lodge.

For the revised, more solemn and dignified ritual, we owe a debt of gratitude to one Rev. George S. Gassner, who was pivotal in composing it. It draws mainly on the first book of Kings, Chapter 5, verses 1 through 10, and the second book of Chronicles, Chapter 2, verses 8 and 9. While plenty of other Masonic ritual also places prominence on the story of the construction of the first temple, this piece focuses on the craftsmen that Hiram, King of Tyre, sent into the forests of Lebanon to fell and hew the timber for the project.

Upon Corson's passing in 1879, the ritual was preserved and sustained by Dr. Stevens, who coordinated the first degree team and continued to perform the work across the Garden State. Apparently, the epicenter at that time was Glassboro, NJ, where this degree team arrived in 1887 to confer the work on fifteen candidates. In 1901, fifty-four members who had been initiated thus far convened to bestow the degree upon fifty-three candidates from Glassboro, Clayton, Williamstown, Mantua, Woodbury, and Philadelphia. In 1902, the charter members convened in Trenton, NJ, to formally organize the Tall Cedars of Lebanon of America. The organization retained this name until 1971 when they instituted a

Forest in Canada, thus becoming the Tall Cedars of Lebanon of North America.

While the Tall Cedars supported a variety of charitable causes in our earlier history, we decided in 1951 to focus our contributions and efforts on muscular dystrophy. In the beginning, this was directed to the metabolism unit of the research center in NYC. When that closed in 1972, we redirected our resources to the Muscular Dystrophy Association, along with the Jerry Lewis Tall Cedar Day Camp in the summer season. The partnership with MDA continues to this day, and locally we support YMCA's Camp Kon-o-kwee Spencer for special needs in the summer.

In 1979, Essex Forest No. 8 of New Jersey (which no longer exists) established a program selling roses as a new fundraiser for the Tall Cedars. A total of $5,261 was raised that first year. "Roses Against Muscular Dystrophy" was adopted as a national program and offered on street corners and at special events of the Forests. The program continues to this day, although commonly artificial roses are sold.

Since around 2002, Tall Cedars have also sold teddy bears to raise funds for the Muscular Dystrophy Foundation. The program was created by Earl Myers, who was Supreme Tall Cedar at the time. Recently, the design changes every year, making them a collector's item; the emblem and colors are selected by the Supreme Tall Cedar and used on other promotional items for the year.

Regarding the local chapter, our very own Pittsburgh Forest No. 160 was originally located in Turtle Creek and was very active with over 200 members. They not only had their regular membership but had the Ranger unit (which is a marching unit with uniforms, like an honor guard, that also participated in ritual), and a Cedarette unit for women. They always went to all the conventions when they were in Atlantic City, Ocean City, and Baltimore. They buddied up with Wa-Cha-Gree Forest No. 149 (named for Washington, Charleroi, and Greensburg) and went together. John Sanders from 149 would make a float for the parade almost every year, and often won prizes. Pittsburgh Forest No. 160 also used to have a bagpipe band that played at our events and also for the Shrine.

There's a small article in the Pittsburgh Press from October 20, 1964, regarding the making of a "Cedar At Sight" (a term used for expedited initiation), for the benefit of former Pittsburgh Pirate Dick Groat. Groat, who was born in Wilkinsburg, was signed to the Pirates just days after graduating from Duke, and played for Pittsburgh from 1952 to 1962 when he was traded to the St. Louis Cardinals.

There was a member by the name of John C. Sarver, who was Grand Tall Cedar of the Pittsburgh Forest in 1969 and went on to become Supreme Tall Cedar (leading the national governing body) in 1975. Throughout the 1970s and 1980s, Pittsburgh Forest was at its peak in activity and membership. However, in 1999, their building was destroyed by flooding, including ritual costumes and many books and records. When they moved from Turtle Creek to Pittsburgh, much of the membership who were elderly did not want to make the trip into town and membership declined.

Today, Pittsburgh Forest No. 160 meets the first Wednesday of varying months at the discretion of the presiding officer—roughly quarterly—at the Greater Pittsburgh Masonic Center. We have a small but enthusiastic membership (forty-one members as of June 2018), which takes the dual missions of fostering fellowship among all Masons and supporting muscular dystrophy research very much to heart.

CONCLUSION

In several of these bodies I have joined over the past twelve years, I am happy to see the same faces in multiple settings, as well as some fellows who only belong to one or the other. Each group does a tremendous amount to support one form of philanthropy or another. Some groups focus more on conduct and philosophy while others focus on fellowship and entertainment, and most, a nurturing balance of the two. All of them have a rich and colorful history, which it has been my great pleasure to share with you this evening. I hope the presentation has satisfied some curiosity for you; although, if it has stimulated you to seek even further, all the better.

www.ingramcontent.com/pod-product-compliance
Lightning Source LLC
Chambersburg PA
CBHW051501050726

47593CB00005B/2165